*This book is dedicated to
Anna Hayford and Michael Omartian,
without whom life would be incomplete.*

# Acknowledgments

With special thanks:

To Susan Martinez, for being the best office manager, listening ear, advice giver, faithful supporter, prayer partner, precious sister, and eternal friend.

To Anna Hayford, for your strength, constancy, wisdom, love, sense of humor, and rock-solid faith.

To Michael Omartian, for your love, faithfulness, and time spent cooking all those great meals so this book could be finished.

To Roz Thompson, Susan Martinez, and Amanda Omartian, for all your strong and faith-filled prayers.

To Bob Hawkins Jr., Carolyn McCready, Teresa Evenson, Julie McKinney, LaRae Wiekert, Mary Cooper, Terry Glaspey, John Constance, Betty Fletcher, Kim Moore, Peggy Wright, and the entire Harvest House family, for all your kindness, encouragement, and support.

# Contents

Where two or three are gathered together
in My name, I am there in the midst of them.

MATTHEW 18:20

# A Message
# for Our
# Time

You may be asking yourself, "Why are Stormie Omartian and Pastor Jack Hayford writing a book together on prayer? They have each separately written books on prayer for years."

Actually, I (Stormie) have been asking *myself* that question. Only I put it a little differently. *Why would Pastor Jack Hayford consent to write a book with me? He doesn't need me or anyone else, and I feel unworthy to have my name on the cover of the same book. He has written books on prayer that make me reticent to say that I have too, because they are so great.*

The multiplied hundreds of thousands of us who know Pastor Jack agree that he is one of the best Bible teachers in the world today. We who sat under his teaching have a common bond of love for the Lord, a clear understanding of God's Word and His ways, and a deep and lasting love for Pastor Jack. Every time I speak anywhere, I tell the story of how I met the Lord. When I mention Pastor Jack's name, people in the audience always respond with cheering, clapping, or sighing. I was recently giving a talk in a place where I didn't speak the language, so I was communicating through an interpreter. When I mentioned

Pastor Jack's name, the same thing happened, only with a three-second delay. Obviously the Pastor Jack effect is universal.

In terms of energy, Jack Hayford has a supernatural gift that enables him to leave the rest of us in the dust. When my husband and I went to the Holy Land with him and his wife, Anna, along with a group from our church, we fondly called it the We-Ran-Today-Where-Jesus-Walked Tour. While I do one book, he does three. In the time it takes me to write and prepare one talk, he does a hundred sermons. This is no average person, although he would disagree.

I could write 15 books on the things I learned from Pastor Jack over the 23 years I spent under his teaching at Church on the Way. Actually, come to think of it, I already have. Each of the books I have written are in some part born out of what I learned there. Pastor Jack is mentioned and quoted in nearly every book.

I've talked about his profound influence on my life since the beginning of my public ministry. He was more than just my pastor; he was and still is my spiritual father. He taught me to love Jesus, to worship God, and to be led by the work of the Holy Spirit in all that I do. And he taught me how to pray. I sat under his teaching for three years before I married my husband, Michael, and then together we grew under Pastor Jack's input for 20 more years before moving to another state where the Lord was calling us to put all we had learned into practice.

So why, if Pastor Jack has written so much on prayer already, would we need to write a book together? Couldn't someone just go out and buy all 45 of Jack Hayford's books and not bother with this one? Yes, you could and you would only be the better for it. But I believe, and so does Pastor Jack, that this is a book for our time. Today! It contains a message for all of us in the body of Christ that we must hear loud and clear. It is crucial to our future and the future of the next generation. God wants our collective prayers to move His hand in the world in accordance with His will. But that can only happen if we pray together in unity and by the power of the Holy Spirit.

Because I had never written anything with someone else before, I asked Pastor Jack how he envisioned we should do this book. He said immediately and emphatically, "*You* are writing the book. I'll send you my tapes and books on the subject to refresh your memory, and you tell me wherever you think I can provide added help."

So that's what I have done. I've listened to Pastor Jack's tapes again, reread some of his books, and had two meetings with him to ask questions so he can fill in the blanks. We've also had extensive chapter-by-chapter interaction on the telephone, as this has been a genuine team effort. I have shared here what I learned from him on the subject of prayer over the last 30 years, and how I saw it worked out practically and powerfully in my life and the lives of others. And I've asked the Holy Spirit to help me communicate all this in a way that will enable each of us to move in power when we pray.

Because Pastor Jack and the Holy Spirit have taught me everything I know on prayer, it's only fitting that the three of us should write this book together—Pastor Jack and I and, shall we say, a Ghostwriter?

— *Stormie Omartian*

# One

# What Is the Power and How Do I Get It?

The first time I met Pastor Jack Hayford, he told me I was ignorant. He didn't say it in a mean way. He was just stating a fact.

I had been singing on a record album that Christian songwriters Jimmy and Carol Owens had written, and we were rehearsing at their home before we went into the studio. I was the only one working on the project who wasn't a Christian. Pastor Hayford came by to see how rehearsals were going, and when we took a break, Jimmy introduced me to him.

The pastor immediately asked me a few questions about my relationship with God and specifically inquired as to whether I knew Jesus. I responded with a mystical spiel about how my occult practices had taught me to commune with a higher power through meditation and belief in a creative force. My New Age explanation did not impress him in the least, and he made some very direct statements about Jesus being Lord and the only way to God.

I didn't buy into any of what he was telling me, and that's when he said I was ignorant. No one had ever told me I was ignorant before. In spite of having come from a miserably abusive childhood, I had for the most part gotten straight A's in school. So even though my opinion of myself was very low, at least I did not think I was ignorant.

He was not at all hostile. In fact, he was careful to explain his choice of words.

"You are an intelligent person, not stupid," he said. "By ignorant I mean you are unknowing of, or ignoring, what it is you need."

His words made me feel better, but the conversation abruptly ended when it was clear I was not open to agreeing with anything he was saying.

Prior to this, my only experience with people who talked about Jesus were those who yelled rudely about Him on street corners and others who appeared to me to live dead and dull lives that I didn't want to emulate. Of course, my mother always talked about Jesus, but she was crazy and mean and made Him sound as crazy and mean as she was. I didn't listen to any of these people because their abrasive and insensitive manner was distasteful to me. Unfortunately, I associated all Christians with them.

I did notice, however, that the Christians I was singing with on these record sessions were quite different. They were loving, kind, peaceful, dynamic, and intelligent—not at all pushy or rude. I was attracted to them because of their manner. Even so, I still was not open to what Pastor Hayford had to say. In fact, I found him to be quite intimidating because he was confident, zealous, and overwhelmingly direct. I certainly didn't want to be around him again if he was going to put me on the spot with such an uncomfortable line of questioning. I fully dismissed him—and all the other Christians—as not as being enlightened as I was. Never mind that *they* seemed happy and *I* was miserable.

The reason I was on that recording session in the first place was because of a friend of mine named Terry. She was one of the best singers I had ever heard, and she was only 20. I was 26. I marveled how at such a young age she could pick up any sheet of music, no matter how difficult, and sight-read it perfectly with great quality and nuance in her voice. She always contracted the sessions we did together, which meant she hired the singers. Not many 20-year-olds were contractors, so I had a great deal of respect for her.

Terry and I had become good friends over two years of doing TV shows and record sessions together. She liked that I would follow her lead and blend my voice with hers instead of trying to compete with it. She talked a lot about her faith in Jesus and the church she attended, but because she wasn't in the room when I met Jack Hayford, I didn't realize he was the pastor of *her* church.

I didn't see Pastor Hayford again until well over a year later. During that time, my life spiraled downhill. All of my fear, anxiety, hopelessness, self-hatred, and emotional pain increased to the point that I became so depressed I could hardly function. Depression was something I had suffered with for many years because I was raised by a mother who was severely mentally ill. She locked me in a closet for much of my early childhood, and that destroyed any sense of self-worth or hope I might have had for my future. Because of the pain, sadness, and despair I felt all of the time, I got into drugs, alcohol, Eastern religions, the occult, and wrong relationships to try and mask it. But these methods only brought temporary relief, and then I was pulled down even lower than before. I eventually hit rock bottom and decided life wasn't worth living anymore.

I had been doing two TV shows a week, which meant I was working 12 to 14 hours a day, seven days a week. It was insanity for anyone to do that, but I was too insecure to turn work down. I was headed for a wall and I knew it, but I didn't know how to stop. My whole life seemed like one mistake, failure, and disaster piled on top of another, and I was exhausted from trying to live as though there wasn't anything wrong. I had tried everything to find a way out of all this pain, but I had failed at that too. I seriously and meticulously planned my suicide and how I could make it look like an accidental drug overdose so my sister and father wouldn't be hurt by it. I knew my mother would barely notice.

When one of my TV shows ended for the season, Terry called me to sing on another record session. While we were sitting next to each other on a break, I shared some of what I was feeling with her. I didn't mention the suicide part, however. Even at this desperate time in my life, I still didn't want anyone to know about my secret plans.

"I can see you are not doing well," Terry said. "Why don't you come with me and meet my pastor? He is amazing, and I know he can help you."

She had been telling me more and more about her faith in God every time we were together, but she did it in such a gentle and appealing way that I wasn't put off by it. In fact, I was attracted to the lifestyle she embraced. She seemed to always be full of life, purpose, and clarity and totally without the condemnation and self-judgment that was so crippling to me. But I still considered myself too educated and intellectual to actually believe something so absurd as what she was talking about. She said that a man named Jesus, who called Himself the Son of God, died for me so that all my sins could be erased and I would have eternal life with Him.

*Yeah, sure,* I thought to myself. *And where do Santa Claus and the Easter Bunny come in? Right after the Tooth Fairy, perhaps?*

Even though it seemed to me that Terry and the others on the recording sessions had rather quaint and unenlightened beliefs, I recognized that they were certainly nice people and they had a distinctly pure, simple, sweet, loving, and uncomplicated spirit about them.

*If only I could fall for something so outlandish and my brain could be as numb to stark reality as theirs,* I thought.

As bad off as I was at that moment, I still hesitated to respond positively to Terry's request. But this time she pushed me harder on the subject than she had ever done before.

"What have you got to lose, Stormie?" she asked with urgency in her voice. "Just come meet him."

I paused for a momentary look in the mirror of my life, and what I saw looking back at me was shockingly fragile and dark. Was I on the brink of self-destruction and still refusing a hand that could possibly pull me out of the quicksand into which I was sinking? Realizing that I had nothing to lose because I had nothing to start with, I finally said, "Okay, I'll go meet him."

Terry made arrangements to pick me up at my house a few days later and take me to meet her pastor at a popular restaurant nearby. She was astute enough to not trust me to get there on my own. When we arrived, he was already waiting for us at a table.

"This is Jack Hayford," she said as she introduced us. "But everyone calls him Pastor Jack."

He extended his hand warmly and smiled, and I did the same.

I thought he seemed familiar, but I didn't recall that earlier meeting and apparently he didn't either. In fact, I would not remember that this was the same man until well over a year later.

After the waitress took our order, Pastor Jack asked me a few questions about myself. I was beyond the point of trying to put up a good front, so I shared with him how I was feeling. Of course, I left out the part about my suicide plans and my crazy mother. It would be a long time before I would ever reveal anything to anyone about either of those things.

I told him I'd had a hard time getting up that morning because of my severe depression, which had become a daily, gut-wrenching battle. I had put in 16 hard hours at CBS studios the previous day and night taping the *Glen Campbell Show,* where I worked as a singer, dancer, and actress. I was exhausted and discouraged and willing to hear anything that sounded like a reason to live.

When Pastor Jack talked about the Lord, I hung on every word. Right away I had this vague sensation of hope, even though it was very foreign to me. The three of us ate and talked for nearly two hours, and then he asked Terry to drive me to his office at the church so he could give me three books.

"Read these and come by the office next week to tell me what you think about them," he instructed me kindly.

I said I would and secretly postponed my suicide plans another week.

That same day I started reading one of the books and was hooked. I even took the books to work with me and read them when I had down time. Each book talked about things I was totally unfamiliar with, but they all made sense to me.

One book was on the reality of evil and the ways of the devil. It was exactly what I needed to hear, because my occult practices taught me that there was no outside evil force. They said that all evil originates in your mind and comes only from within you. This meant if you could control your mind to think only good thoughts, nothing bad would happen to you. The difficulty with that was when bad things *did* happen to me, I had to blame it all on myself. And the weight of that load was too heavy for my shoulders to carry. It only exacerbated my sense of failure. On the other hand, this book Pastor Jack gave me showed how to distinguish between *my sin,* which I was responsible for, and the *enemy's plan* to destroy, which was not my fault. It revealed how I could triumph victoriously over the plans of evil and fulfill *God's* plan for my life instead.

The second book was on the power of the Holy Spirit. This intrigued me so much because I had never heard of such a thing. I loved reading about how receiving Jesus as Savior meant that God's Holy Spirit would come and live in me and transform me from the inside out. If this was really true, I wanted that more than anything in the world.

The third book was actually the Gospel of John from the Bible in book form. It explained who Jesus was...and *is*...and how He provided a way for me to be set free from all my sin and failure. I could receive an infusion of life by believing in Him, and He would give me the power to live His way. Every word of it fed my spirit and spoke life to my soul. I had read small parts of the Bible before, but it never meant much to me beyond being interesting history, nice poetry, and an example of literature from that time. But now, for reasons I could not understand, my eyes were opened to it and every word came alive. It wasn't until months later that I realized it was because people were praying for me to be able to discern the truth about the things of God.

When Terry took me back to Pastor Jack's office the following week, he asked me what I thought of the books.

"I believe they are the truth," I answered.

He then asked me if I wanted to receive Jesus as my Savior, and I said yes. When he and Terry prayed for me, I felt a surge of peace. I didn't know for sure what I had done, but I cancelled my suicide plans and felt hope for the first time that I could remember.

At Pastor Jack's suggestion, I started attending church every Sunday morning with Terry and her husband. From the first service I attended at Church On The Way, I felt completely at home.

The church was an old-fashioned small white chapel with a tall steeple, like the kind often seen on Christmas cards. The only thing missing was the snow. But there was nothing old about what was going on inside. It over-flowed with new life. The sanctuary was packed as full as it could possibly get with people of all ages, colors, sizes, and shapes. Extra chairs were brought in and placed in every available space, even up on the platform and behind the pulpit.

The moment I walked in, I felt a strong, loving, com-forting, healing, and freeing presence. It was so thick and soul-stirring that I cried through nearly the entire service. And I wasn't the only one who felt that way. I came to learn that what we all sensed in that place was the love of God and the presence of His Holy Spirit. It was like nothing I had ever experienced before, and it brought such healing and restoration to my life that I changed in some amazing and undeniable way each time I went there.

The worship part of the service was life-transforming. Whatever hardness of heart I may have brought in with me soon melted away, and all anxiety and fear was replaced by joy. We worshiped God for nearly an hour, but the time flew by. Every worship song, praise chorus, or hymn we sang brought freedom in my soul, and years of uncried tears fell like refreshing rain through each one.

Pastor Jack got up to teach from the Bible, and he was the greatest speaker I had ever heard. He was insightful and thought-provoking, not boring or unclear, and I hung on every word. He made the Scriptures come alive to my understanding, and every verse became immediately relevant to my life.

I could feel myself growing in the things of God each week. My eyes were opening to a world I never knew existed. A world where anything was possible, because I was learning how to walk with and pray to the *God* of the *impossible.*

I found out that if I wanted my prayers answered, I didn't just send up a list to God as though He was a great Santa Claus in the sky. There was something required of me. I had to get my life cleaned up and set on the right track. I needed to be reading the Word of God and living in obedience to God's ways. The good news was that I didn't have to make it all happen by myself. The Holy Spirit in me would *teach* me all things and *enable* me to live the way I should. Understanding the Holy Spirit was key to seeing the power of God move in response to my prayers.

## Finding Your Keys

What I liked about Pastor Jack's teachings was the way he illustrated the points he was making in a way that made it easy for me to understand. His pictures stuck with me because they related to my life. In one of my favorite of his illustrations, he compared the power of prayer to the engine of a car.

"There is very little power in the key that fits my car," he said. "The car engine has power, but it does not come to life without my key being put into the ignition. In other words, I don't have the power to go outside and get myself going 60 miles an hour, but I have access to a resource that can get me moving at that speed. Jesus said, 'I will give you the keys of the kingdom of heaven' (Matthew 16:19). Keys mean the authority, the privilege, the access. Some things will not be turned on unless *you* turn them on. Some things will not be turned loose unless *you* turn them loose. Some things will not be set free unless *you* set them free. The key doesn't make the power of the engine, it *releases* the power of the engine."

I understood that having legal possession of the keys to a car was evidence that we have the *right* to that car. In the same way, because Jesus gives us the keys of His kingdom, we have the right to come before God in prayer. "As many as received Him, to them He gave the right to become children of God" ( John 1:12). As His children we have the right to come before our heavenly Father in prayer.

Having the keys to the car also means that we have the *responsibility* for it. In that same way, we are responsible for our side of the partnership with God in prayer. If we don't use the key of prayer, then nothing is likely to happen. There won't be anything released or unlocked.

Our problem is we sometimes forget where we put the keys to our car. The same is true in our prayer life. We misplace the key that unlocks God's power. We come upon a situation...or a situation comes upon us...and we forget to use our key of prayer to move powerfully in and through it. Whenever I lose the keys to my car, I ask God to show me where they are and help me to find them. He always does. Whenever we lose sight of our prayer key, we can ask Him to help us find it again. He will do that too.

## Starting the Engine

A key is no good to us if we never use it to unlock anything. If the car key doesn't connect with the ignition, the power of the engine will not be ignited. God's power is always available to us, but if we don't use the key of prayer, we can't appropriate this power for our lives.

Have you ever wondered why there are good people who love God, read His Word, and pray, but they don't see His power move in response to their prayers? Why their life doesn't affect or change the world around them for His kingdom, and so the world looks upon their faith as being irrelevant? It's because there is a misunderstanding of the need to ask for the Holy Spirit's power. The precious Holy Spirit enters every believer, but He only moves in power in those who invite His overflowing enablement. Those who *don't* invite him are like cars that have fuel in the tank, but the engine has not been turned on.

People often hesitate to pray because they do not understand the power of the Holy Spirit working through them when they do. Or they don't believe that God's power is there for *them*. Too often we think the power in prayer is not attainable for the average person like us. But God says it is available to all who love Him with their whole being and love others as themselves.

There is an important correlation between God's love and God's power. Jesus said, "A new commandment I give to you, that you love one another; as I have loved you, that you also love one another" (John 13:34).

"If you're going to function as a person of the kingdom, then there are certain regulations you need to live in," explained Pastor Jack. "The foundational law of the kingdom is the law of love. It's not a casual 'feel good-ism.' It is the love of God poured forth in our hearts (Romans 5:5). The fountainhead of all power is that flow of the divine love of God happening in us. Loving others is a kingdom law, and you can't get kingdom action without obeying kingdom laws. His keys don't fit our private kingdom. His power is unleashed upon command, but not for our personal gain."

He didn't mean we don't benefit from God's power. We certainly do. Every day. Whenever we acknowledge that we need a fresh flow of God's power working in us and ask for God's Holy Spirit to flow through us as we pray, we will see His power move in our lives. But He wants us to recognize that His Spirit is love. And if we want a demonstration of God's power, then God's love must be the motivating force behind everything we do and each prayer we pray.

In order to move into that kind of love-motivated praying, however, our first step must be to submit ourselves to God and wait at His feet in prayer. It's not that He is trying to keep His power *from* us, it's that He wants us to depend on *Him* for it.

After Jesus was resurrected, He visited His disciples and said, "I send the Promise of My Father upon you; but tarry in the city of Jerusalem until you are endued with power from on high" (Luke 24:49). Jesus was telling them to wait where they were until they had what they needed for what was ahead of them.

Pastor Jack likened this to the clothing that we wear. "Jesus is saying don't go forth until you have the necessary clothing that prepares you for what's ahead."

When I first heard this, a vision crystallized clearly in my mind. I saw the nakedness of a person who prays without being clothed in God's power and then wonders why they don't get their prayers answered. It's one thing to be clothed with the righteousness of God through the blood of Jesus Christ when we are born again. And that's what we need in order to stand before God in perfect confidence. But we also need to be clothed with power for the purpose of being what we're made to be on this earth.

"Just like we are to be clothed with the armor of God for spiritual warfare," Pastor Jack told us. "Jesus is saying He doesn't want us going naked into a world that needs us to be prepared with what is necessary in order for us to make a difference there."

God's power is made available to us in order to do two things. One is to accomplish God's purposes here on earth. The other is to give evidence to people around us that Jesus is alive. But we can't do either of those things if we pray without being clothed with the power from heaven. Without the power of the Holy Spirit, we are praying uncovered.

If you're like me, you would never say to God, "I don't need Your power. I can live my life just fine all by myself, so don't try to do anything in me or through me." Yet there are many people who do that every day. Maybe not in those exact words, but they do it by failing to open up to one of the greatest gifts God has ever given to us: the gift of His Holy Spirit. When we understand that this key of prayer is in our hands, and it can ignite God's power when it connects with the Holy Spirit in us, we will unlock and unleash the power of God in our lives like nothing we have ever seen before.

## Unleashing the Power

The first time I heard Pastor Jack speak, he was teaching from the book of Exodus and it fascinated me. I could hardly wait to get to church each week to hear more. I finally went out and bought my own Bible, like he had suggested, so I could read ahead and find out what was going to happen next.

I especially wanted to know more about the Israelites being delivered out of Egypt and moving into the Promised Land. I realized that I, too, had been living in bondage in Egypt and needed to be delivered out of it. When he talked about the Israelites wandering around in the wilderness for 40 years because of their disobedience, I knew I didn't want to be wandering around in any wilderness because I wasn't obeying God. I had been in a wilderness for far too long already. I wanted to get free of anything that kept me from moving into the promised land of all God had for me.

One of the things I wanted to get free of was depression.

On a recording session I did with Terry before I received the Lord, she introduced me to a young, talented musician named Michael. I had the opportunity to get acquainted with him on this short series of record sessions, but I didn't see much of him after they were over. He was a Christian and I wasn't. We lived in different worlds.

Two years and a lifetime later, after I came to know the Lord, we ran into each other one Sunday morning at the church. I had been going there for a few months, and that was his first time there. Not long after that we started dating and were married about a year later.

I thought being married would bring the kind of security that would pull me out of the depressions I had suffered with for years. But it didn't. Getting free was obviously not going to happen through some outside event. It was going to have to be an inside job.

I knew my depression wasn't clinical because medicine didn't help me at all. I had been to psychiatrists, and no amount of drugs could make me forget the things my mother had said to me—that I was worthless, useless, purposeless, a failure, and no good. By this point in my life I realized my mother was not sane, but I still struggled unbearably with believing that what she said about me was the truth. Even though I had been out of her house for ten years, I still heard those tapes playing over and over in my head. When it was evident I wasn't getting free of these periodic blackout times of depression no matter what I did, I became even more depressed.

*What is wrong with me?* I asked the Lord. *I have Jesus in my heart, an eternal future with You, a husband who loves me, and financial security for the first time in my life. Why can't I get free of depression?*

At my husband's suggestion, I went to a counselor in the church who was extremely gifted in the things of God. Her name was Mary Anne, and she was the wife of one of the pastors. She had great knowledge of God's power to deliver people from bondage. She instructed me to fast and pray for three days and said she would fast with me. I thought that was an amazing sacrifice from someone I had never met before.

When I came back to her office after the fast, she had me do three things. First of all, I had to confess all my sins that I could think of, which was frightening because I had done so many wrong things in my life. Secondly, I had to renounce all my occult practices. Even though I had stopped practicing these things after I came to know the Lord, I had never actually renounced them. Thirdly, I had to confess any unforgiveness I had—especially toward my mother. After I had done those things, Mary Anne and another pastor's wife laid their hands on my head and shoulders and prayed.

The moment they prayed for me to be set free from depression, I felt an unmistakable surge through my body and hands that was like an electrical current. It was not like anything I had ever felt before. Immediately I had the distinct and undeniable sensation of a great burden being lifted off of my entire being. Afterward I felt light and free. And I was no longer depressed.

Depression was something I had struggled with as far back as I could remember, so it was hard for me to believe it was really gone. In fact, to illustrate the weakness of my faith, I fully expected the depression to return the next morning. And if it had, I would still have been happy to be free of it for even a day. However, when I awoke the next morning, the depression was still gone. As it was the following day. And the day after that. And the next. To my astonishment, it never came back again.

I'm not saying I never experienced depression again, because many depressing things happen in life. But whenever I did feel depression, it was because of a particular circumstance or attack of the enemy and not just an old familiar feeling. And I was always able to go to God and get free of it right away. From the moment that paralyzing depression was broken in my life, I was a firm believer in the power of God working through faith-filled people who pray.

"The Holy Spirit is the one, who by His presence flowing in our lives, generates the power in us," Pastor Jack explained. "When we pray, we are opening an avenue for the release of His power. The Holy Spirit brings the power of God into our lives and enables us to be the conduit of it. We become like a lightning rod as we transmit that power in prayer."

Once you experience the power of God unleashed in your life through prayer, you will never be the same. Nor will you settle for anything less.

## Driving Under His Influence

If you are wanting to move into new territory in your life, it is imperative that you decide exactly who is in the driver's seat. Is it going to be you, or is it going to be God? Are you going to head out on your own, or are you willing to let Him lead you? Will you be moving in the flesh, or will you be empowered by the Holy Spirit? It's important to make that crucial decision, because it will determine how effectively you pray.

Jesus *always* moved under the Holy Spirit's influence. His disciples observed that. They personally witnessed

Him healing people, casting out demons, and performing many other miracles, and they wanted to know how these things happened. They recognized that Jesus had a source of power they didn't have. They also saw Him frequently go to a private place and pray, and whenever He did, the life and power of God would be infused in Him. They obviously knew there was a connection between power and prayer, because they didn't ask Him to teach them how to get power. They asked Him to teach them how to pray. And what He taught them is now known as the Lord's Prayer (Matthew 6:9-13; Luke 11:2-4).

"In everything Jesus did on earth, He did not depend on His own resources and power as God," Pastor Jack explained. "Though He was God, He chose to walk as a human being. When the Son of God became flesh, He laid aside His divine prerogatives as God and became entirely dependent upon the resources of the Holy Spirit. He did all this voluntarily, never becoming less than God, but in humility chose to walk among us as a human being" (Philippians 2:5-8).

This is the most amazing thing to me! Even though Jesus was the Son of God, He still went to His Father in prayer in order to receive power for all He needed to do. And He teaches us how to do the same. God wants us to draw on His resources by coming to Him in prayer and seeking a fresh infusion of power the way Jesus did.

"Jesus didn't teach His disciples the Lord's Prayer so they would have something to recite over and over," explained Pastor Jack. "He was teaching them how to release the power they needed. He said the way to pray is to first recognize that God is your Father. ('Our Father in heaven.') That's the grounds for the relationship. Second, worship Him. ('Hallowed be Your name.') Then, on the basis of the relationship His grace has bestowed on us and the worship which is due His great name, we are directed to pray with boldness. ('Your kingdom come, Your will be done on earth as it is in heaven.') These words invoke at earth level what God has ordained at heaven level."

Many people think praying "Your kingdom come" is a prayer about sometime in the future. But it is not a someday prayer. Just like "give us this day our daily bread, and forgive us our debts" is not talking about someday in the future. It is referring to now. When we pray "Your kingdom come," we are asking God's kingdom to invade our circumstances right now.

Just like Jesus, we need to be empowered by the Holy Spirit in all that we do. He is our Teacher, Helper, and Guide, and we must ask Him to teach us how to pray with fervency and passion so that our prayers have power. We must request that He help us have love and compassion for others, even those who are hard to love, so that our prayers are rightly motivated. We must invite Him to be in the driver's seat of our lives so that He can guide us where we need to go. When we move through each day under His influence, we will accomplish things we would otherwise never be able to do.

## Navigating the Danger Zones

There are three roads to travel in life: the way of self, the way of Satan, and the way of God. We have a choice as to which road we will take. And it's highly dangerous to make the wrong choice.

If we go the devil's way, it leads to darkness, destruction, and death because he is a thief who comes to steal, to kill, and to destroy. If we choose our own way, nothing will turn out as good as it could have in our lives. Plus, we will eventually end up going Satan's way, because he is the originator of having it your own way. But if we go *God's* way, we will end up in a realm that brings life and hope because it gives us power over self and Satan.

One of the dangers we must look out for when traveling through life is forgetting who we are and where we are going. The day we were born again, we received new citizenship papers! Our name was written in the Lamb's Book of Life. We were registered in heaven. We are now traveling with papers proving that we were born into God's kingdom and we represent a higher authority and power than any force of hell.

"As wonderful as that endowment of authority is, though, we need to keep perspective," warned Pastor Jack. "Remember, when the disciples were thrilled about being able to cast out demons, Jesus told them that this was not the thing to get excited about. He said they should get excited that their names were registered in heaven, because that meant the grounds of their authority were secured through God's throne—His kingdom—and that's why the power of hell could not prevail against them."

We need to always keep focused on that truth as well.

In Tennessee, where I now live, there are many narrow, winding, two-lane roads. On either side of these roads are drainage ditches that have been made deep by torrents of rain over the years. When driving there you must be diligent to keep your eyes on the road because there is no margin for error. It's the same in our spiritual lives. We must keep our eyes on who we are in the Lord and where we are headed. There is little margin for error on this road too.

We must be especially mindful of this on days when things are going well. In Tennessee the trees are brilliant with red, yellow, and gold in the fall, or breathtaking with pink, lavender, and white in the spring. When we start focusing on the beauty instead of the road, it's easy to end up stuck in a ditch. That's what happened to the Israelites. Every time things started going well, they forgot to keep their focus on God and instead became sidetracked with their own interests. And remember what happens when you start doing your *own* thing? Before you know it, you're doing the *devil's* thing, and that leads to a crisis.

Some people are crisis "pray-ers." They don't pray for good health until something bad comes back from a medical test. They don't pray for safety and protection until they have an accident. They only pray when things go wrong. But you can end up going off a cliff when you navigate life like that. Once you understand the power and authority you have in prayer, you will find yourself praying all the time about everything.

It has been said that Satan trembles when he sees the weakest saint upon his knees. That's not because he is afraid of *us*. It's because he knows that the power of God gives us victory over the works of darkness when we pray. That's why we have to keep praying in the good times as well as the bad, no matter what season of life we are in or what road we are on.

## Arriving at Your Destination

Moving forward with Jesus always calls us upward in prayer. Our constancy and consistency in prayer increases as we grow in our understanding of why prayer is so important. Essentially, it has to do with the power God invests in us—the power to touch His throne in heaven from our place on earth. This is most clearly expressed in Jesus' teaching about prayer. And it centers around His well-known words "Your kingdom come. Your will be done on earth as it is in heaven" (Matthew 6:10).

"The kingdom of God is the entire realm of God's universal rule," explained Pastor Jack. "It is also a realm where the reign of God is working in our lives. That means that while our ultimate destination is with Him in heaven, we also have an interim destination—a place and purpose on earth, advancing His heavenly kingdom's purposes. Prayer is pivotal to our fulfilling that place and purpose for us, here and now. It works this way.

"First, when we received Jesus, we are born into that realm—the kingdom of God. That means that even though we live in a realm called 'earth' (say, Denver, Dallas, Boston, or wherever), we have the privilege and power to function as citizens of another realm—God's kingdom. We have literally been made a 'new creation' in Christ the King, and have exited the kingdom of darkness to live in the kingdom of God's Son (see Colossians 1:13-14; 2 Corinthians 5:17).

"Second, as newborn citizens of God's 'in heaven' kingdom, Jesus teaches us to pray, 'Your kingdom come. Your will be done, on earth as it is in heaven' (Matthew 6:10). The depth and power of that prayer are too seldom grasped.

"Hear that, loved ones. Our victorious Savior has told us to call on our almighty Father. He is showing us that the way God has willed for things on earth to be changed begins with His people here—you and me—inviting heaven into the mix. In short, by His own choice He has limited His will, ways, or works to those places on earth they are invited. Prayer is the privileged role we have been given to issue the invitation to His almightiness—penetrating earth's realm of brokenness with His heavenly kingdom's saving health and wholeness."

This doesn't mean that God's ultimate rule on earth through His Son is up to us. He has appointed a day when that shall occur. But He has directed, to use His words, that we "do business until I come" (Luke 19:13). He has made it clear that prayer is the primary "business" of His people. It is the way transformation is brought about.

"Nothing in all of Jesus' teaching is clearer about the place of prayer in the advancement of His kingdom purposes on earth than when He taught us how to pray 'Your kingdom come,' " said Pastor Jack. "In short, He is saying, 'Until I come again to introduce My ultimate rule on earth, the Father's rule and power waits to be invited into your own and other human situations.' "

How well we understand and accept this privilege and responsibility we have in prayer will determine how much of God's power will penetrate our world. As Pastor Jack says, "All power in heaven and earth is *His*—but all prayer invoking heaven's power into earth's need is *ours*."

It is God's will to wait for our invitation. If we pray and invite God's sovereign power to manifest in earth's suffering and pain, then He will move in power. Then His kingdom will enter our lives and our circumstances and work on earth what He has willed in heaven. When we understand this, it will inspire us to pray as we have never prayed before.

∽ ∽ ∽

God wants to use us for His kingdom purposes. And that's what we want as well. We don't want to just read *about* God, we want His life *in* us. We want His anointing *upon* us in such a way that when people see us or talk to us, they see that Jesus is alive. We want people to be attracted to Jesus because of what they see of Him in us.

When God brought the Israelites out of Egypt, He told them that if they would walk His way, He would make them a kingdom of priests. And they would be a people who moved in a realm of authority that was related to their priesthood. They would have a relationship with the One who was the head of the kingdom. But Israel lost that opportunity because they didn't want what God wanted. As a result, they never arrived where God intended for them to go. But *we* can arrive where God intends for us to go because we *do* want what God wants (1 Peter 2:5-9).

God wants to pour out His Spirit upon each of us and enable us to become ambassadors of His kingdom. He wants to take people who are willing to surrender their lives to Him and show them how to live by the power of His Spirit. We want that as well, because we know we will never be able to pray effectively unless we move in the power that gives evidence of God's presence in our lives. The world around us is too frightening, dangerous, and unpredictable to not be certain that we have access to a power that can make a major difference when we pray.

## Prayer Power

Lord, I realize I am powerless to do anything of significance or accomplish anything lasting without You. I know it is not by my strength or wisdom that powerful things happen in my life, but it is by Your Spirit. My prayers are not answered because of *what* I know, but because of *who* I know. And I am grateful that I know You. Thank You for saving me, Jesus, and setting me free from all that would keep me from moving into everything You have for me. Thank You for filling me with Your Holy Spirit.

Holy Spirit, I acknowledge You this day as my source of power. I invite You to fill me afresh and flow freely through me. I know that without You I can do nothing. I rely on You to do beyond all that I can think or imagine. Teach me in all things. Help me to understand the exceeding greatness of Your power toward us who believe (Ephesians 1:19).

Lord, I don't ever want to become like the people Your Word speaks of who have a form of godliness but deny its power (2 Timothy 3:5). I want to be a person who moves in Your power and whose prayers have the power to effect significant change in the world around me. Help me to always remember to live by the power of Your Spirit and not try to do things in my own strength. Show me how to use the keys You have given me to unlock and unleash Your power in prayer.

You are awesome above all else on the earth. It is You, O Lord, who gives strength and power to Your people (Psalm 68:35). Thank You that Your power is mighty in us. Thank You that just as You raised Jesus from the dead, You will also raise me up by Your power (1 Corinthians 6:14). "When I am old and grayheaded, O God, do not forsake me, until I declare Your strength to this generation, Your power to everyone who is to come" (Psalm 71:18). Thank You that Your grace is sufficient for me. That Your strength is made perfect in my weakness. I would rather boast in my infirmities, so that the power of Christ rests upon me (2 Corinthians 12:9). God, You are my strength and power. You make my way perfect. You make my feet like the feet of deer, and You set me on high places (2 Samuel 22:33-34).

Heavenly Father, I exalt You above all things. May Your kingdom come this day and Your will be done on earth as it is in heaven. Enable me to be a great ambassador of Your kingdom. May people love You more because of what they see of You in me. In Jesus' name I pray.

᠅  ᠅  ᠅

## Word Power

The message of the cross is foolishness to
those who are perishing, but to us who are
being saved it is the power of God.

1 CORINTHIANS 1:18

We have this treasure in earthen vessels, that
the excellence of the power may be
of God and not of us.

2 CORINTHIANS 4:7

His divine power has given to us all things that
pertain to life and godliness, through the
knowledge of Him who called us by glory
and virtue, by which have been given to us
exceedingly great and precious promises, that
through these you may be partakers of the
divine nature, having escaped the corruption
that is in the world through lust.

2 PETER 1:3-4

God has power to help and to overthrow.

2 CHRONICLES 25:8

For the kingdom of God is not in
word but in power.

1 CORINTHIANS 4:20

# Two

# The Power — of — One —

One Sunday morning Pastor Jack stood before the congregation and said he wanted to share an area of failing he had in his life. I knew right away it was not going to be an earth-shattering revelation. He was not getting a divorce, and I was sure he had not robbed a bank, murdered anyone, or committed adultery. So I couldn't imagine what he was going to say.

He had always been very candid about his own frailties and humanity, which was one of the things that endeared him to so many. He would share from his heart and experience for the purpose of helping us to grow.

What he told us was that he had been awakened by the alarm and had gotten up to pray when the Lord spoke to his heart saying, "You have forgotten the discipline of daily devotional habit."

*But that's what I am up doing,* he thought.

"I didn't feel that God was mad at me," he told us. "It was more like the Lord had something to teach me. And I understood what God was dealing with me about. I had learned so much about intercession and worship in the immediately preceding years that I was spending less

*intimate* time with Jesus. It was a call to go back to the
childlike basics of presenting myself to the Lord."

It wasn't that Pastor Jack had stopped being a person
of prayer. He prayed all the time. He always responded to
what he called "Holy Spirit-prompted intercession." Whenever the Holy Spirit signaled a prompting to pray, Pastor
Jack stopped whatever he was doing at the time and
prayed about that. He consulted with the Lord regularly
and sought Him for wisdom about everything. He was a
praise and worship person consistently, and he prayed
daily in prayer groups with other people. No one could
have accused Pastor Jack of not being a praying person.
After all, he was in the middle of praying when God spoke
to him about this. But he had lost the essential discipline
of a daily devotional prayer time.

From his teens through college and the early years of
his public ministry, Pastor Jack had learned to be with the
Lord every morning.

"I don't know when it changed," he explained. "I
couldn't tell you an exact time. I didn't one day say that
I'm not going to get up and pray anymore. It just got sporadic and irregular, and finally I'd lost the discipline. But
something has come clear to my understanding, and I am
persuaded that it will never be lost again."

Most of us can relate to what he described. We've all
struggled with maintaining a consistent and regular prayer
time alone with God at some point in our lives. However,
at the time he spoke about it to our congregation, I was
faithfully doing it. I would get up early every day and go
before the Lord to pray with Him alone. It was no struggle
for me then because I had been in such bad shape when I
received the Lord. I had come out of a life of drugs,
alcohol, the occult, depression, fear, anxiety, and unforgiveness, and I knew I couldn't get through a day without
being with God first. Hearing Pastor Jack talk about his

struggle amazed me because I realized if it could happen to him, it could happen to anyone—including me.

And then one day, a long time later, it did.

A few years ago my devotional prayer life began to slip. I had been extremely sick off and on for about five months. Each time I had an attack of nausea, vomiting, and severe stomach pain, my husband took me to the emergency room, but no one could find anything wrong with me. I tried different hospitals, doctors, and specialists, but there were still no answers. Finally in the middle of one very miserable night, I felt something explode in my body so violently that I knew I would die if I didn't get help immediately. My husband rushed me to the hospital again because it was obvious I didn't have time to wait for an ambulance.

In the emergency room I endured a number of excruciating tests, but still no one could find out what was wrong with me. Finally the specialist called in a surgeon who was courageous enough to say, "We don't know what's causing your pain and sickness, but I believe your appendix has ruptured. I'm going to take you into surgery and if I'm wrong, I'll find out what the problem is."

As it turned out, he was right. After I awakened from the anesthetic he told me, "In another hour I would not have been able to save you."

I was in such bad shape that the surgeon had to make a huge vertical incision from the sternum to the pubic bone. And worst of all, he had to leave the incision open rather than sew it up. That's because it had to be opened every day and cleaned out, and tubes had to be left in to keep it draining by means of a special wound vacuum machine. The wound was never sewed up, and it took five months for it to close itself from the inside out.

During those months of illness before the surgery, I had gotten out of the habit of praying first thing in the morning. Because I never felt well, I had to sleep, eat, and work whenever I was able to. The sicker I became, the harder it was to stay on any kind of normal schedule and the more difficult it was to pray consistently. I continued praying for my husband and children and a few close friends and family members, and of course for my healing, but that was about it.

After my appendix ruptured, however, I had difficulty praying anything beyond the "Help me, Jesus! Heal me, Lord!" kind of desperation prayers. The recovery was so gruesome and agonizing that it was hard to concentrate, and many times I wondered if I would ever be able to do anything normal again. But I felt the sustaining prayers of other people lifting me up and keeping me from getting discouraged and losing heart in the midst of it all. I was grateful for them because they carried me through that time.

Two months into my recovery period, however, I suddenly started having the same kind of abdominal pain and nausea I'd had in the months prior to my appendix rupturing. I couldn't believe that after all I had been through, I still had not gotten rid of the problem. Here I was, not even half healed from the first surgery and still not walking well because of a huge gaping hole in my body, and I had to go back into surgery again. This time the doctor had to remove my gallbladder, which he now believed was the problem from the beginning.

My recovery from the second surgery was extremely slow, as if my body were saying, "This was one too many!"

My prayer time and Bible reading had been continually slipping, but after this second surgery, both fell off dramatically. I'd had so much anesthetic and been on so many drugs that it was hard to concentrate. I read the Bible a little every day, but I felt as though I were reading through a thick fog. Plus, I was in so much pain that I couldn't sit up for very long at a time. I felt frail because I couldn't do anything by myself, not even the basics. The extent of my prayer life centered entirely around healing and surviving the day.

Of course, I had to cancel all speaking engagements and book deadlines that year, and I felt guilty about letting so many people down. But Pastor Jack said, "If a soldier is wounded in battle, during his recovery time no one expects him to be out doing daily drills he is in no condition to do. We can become casualties in the spiritual battle sometimes, and though we are still in the army, the agenda is to get well."

I was grateful to still be in God's army.

In spite of the prayers of other people sustaining me through that time, I still felt empty in my spirit. I realized how much I had fallen out of the discipline of being alone with the Lord in prayer every day. And it went beyond having sickness as an excuse. I was completely out of the habit. As a result, I had a hard time hearing God's voice speaking to my soul. I knew that I, like Pastor Jack, had to start learning this discipline all over again.

When I was well enough, I went back and reviewed all that Pastor Jack had taught us that day on devotional prayer. I gained a renewed sense of perspective, and I was reminded of some things I had forgotten along the way. Things I want to share with you in this chapter. The prayers of others are vital and can help us survive, but to really sense the fullness of God's presence in our lives, we have to be alone with Him every day.

You may wonder why I have put a chapter on praying *alone* with God in a book on praying *together* with other people. The reason is that the more time we spend alone with God, the more powerful our prayers will be when we pray with others. It's not that praying with other people is less effective than praying alone. There is great power when we pray in numbers, and convincing you of that is the very reason for writing this book. But praying with other people *without* spending time alone with God will compromise the effectiveness and power of your prayers. In other words, you will be a more effective prayer partner if you have not neglected your time alone with the Lord.

When I used to play the violin, I found that I was a greater asset to the orchestra I played with if I practiced on my own. The more I played alone, the better I was with the group. It's the same way with prayer.

## What Is Prayer, Exactly?

*Prayer is communicating with God.* Each time we pray, we come in contact with God in a profound and life-changing way.

When we face hopeless situations in our relationships, businesses, work, finances, health, emotions, or children, praying to the God of hope can change the situation. When we struggle with such things as unrealized dreams, an unfulfilling life, lack of mental clarity, or emotional pain, we have access to the God who can touch every area of our lives to transform them and bring about wholeness. He wants to reach down and touch *us,* but first we have to reach up and touch *Him* in prayer. When we pray, we're saying, "I know You are real, Lord, and I want to spend time with You."

*Prayer is praising and worshiping God for who He is.* This takes our focus off of ourselves and places it on Him. It positions Him first in our hearts and allows Him full access to our lives. Pastor Jack taught us that there are two sides to prayer. There is the *fellowship side* and the *partnership side.*

"The fellowship side of prayer is when we come just to be with God in the intimacy of relationship," he explained. "The partnership side is when we exercise the responsibilities of partnering with Him to see the reintroduction of His rule into our circumstances. Worship, praise, adoration, and exaltation are an important part of fellowship with God, but it is also a means of partnering with Him to drive back the darkness."

When we pray we're saying, "Lord, You are wonderful, almighty, all-powerful, the God and Creator of all things. I exalt You above everything, and I worship You for who You are."

*Prayer is telling God we love and adore Him.* It's coming humbly before God and speaking to Him the way we would to someone we dearly love. Prayer is telling God how grateful we are that He loved us before we were even aware He existed. When we pray, we're saying, "I love You, Lord, and I thank You for loving me."

*Prayer is telling God we need Him.* When we *don't* pray, it implies that we think we can handle everything on our own. But the truth is we can't handle *anything* on our own. We need God for everything. We need Him to save us, forgive us, heal us, deliver us, fill us, restore us, redeem us, free us, guide us, protect us, lift us above our limitations, and move us into the plans and purposes He has for us. We can't get there without Him. When we pray we're saying, "I can't live without You, Lord. If You don't intervene in my life, nothing good is going to happen."

*Prayer is making our requests known to God.* It's sharing with Him all that is on our hearts, knowing that He cares about each one of those things. God promises to give us all we need, but we still have to ask. Just as He instructs us to ask for our daily bread, we are to come before Him and ask for whatever else we need too.

Prayer is not a last resort, something we turn to when all else fails, a stab at something in the dark, or an exercise in positive thinking to try and make ourselves feel better. Prayer changes things. But we have to talk to God about the things that need to be changed. Prayer is acknowledging that, even though what we are praying for may seem impossible to us, with God all things are possible (Matthew 19:26). When we pray, we're saying, "Lord, I have these needs, and I know You care about them and will hear my requests."

***Prayer is serving God His way.*** It's not just about us getting *our* needs met, although that's an important part of prayer. God's plan is to rule earth through His delegated authority. That's us—we who believe in Him. God wants us to bring His kingdom to bear upon the issues of the earth. God has things for each of us to do, and they start with prayer.

Pastor Jack said, "If we think that a future in heaven is the sum of Christ's gift to us, we will live out a spiritually immature existence, pointed toward heaven, but pointless on earth."

Pastor Jack was never one to be vague about the truth.

"People need to understand why God doesn't just do everything on His own initiative," he said. "It goes back to God giving the responsibility for governing earth's affairs to humankind (Genesis 1:26,28). He ordained that everything on earth would be determined by human choice. 'The heaven, even the heavens, are the LORD's; but the earth He has given to the children of men' (Psalm 115:16). But it only works when man keeps in relationship with God. The will of God and the works and power of God do not simply flow without an invitation into earth's scene. The Lord has transmitted to His people the responsibility of inviting the presence of the kingdom. It's not because

God *can't* do something without us, but because He *won't* do it without us."

Some people believe that God is going to do whatever He is going to do no matter what, so there is no reason to pray. But the truth is there are things God will not do on earth except in answer to prayer.

"There are people who don't like this idea because they don't want the responsibility that it carries with it," said Pastor Jack. "They just want God to do what He's going to do. But God wants to grow up His sons and daughters, and He waits to move where they invite Him to move. That's what He *wants* to do! His decree is clear about this. But we need to be equally clear: This emphasis does not minimize the sovereignty of God. The power is all His! But views of God's sovereignty can overlook His will to involve His children in advancing His redemptive purposes. The Sovereign God Almighty has decreed that what takes place on earth shall be realized through the willing activities of people who submit to His will and invoke His presence and power."

This explains why the earth is in the mess it's in. God has delegated everything to man, and we have reaped what we've sown. God has determined, and chosen to abide by, this sovereign decree: He works on earth in answer to our prayers, and we have neglected to pray.

The good news is that it's never too late to sow the seeds of prayer and gain a different harvest than the seeds of sin and death we have produced in our world. We can invite God's power to enter specific situations right now. When we pray, we're saying "Lord, I want to be Your instrument through which You do what You want to do on this planet. Help me to pray according to Your will, so that *Your* will is done on earth."

This is what it means to pray "Your kingdom come, Your will be done."

## What Makes Praying So Hard Sometimes?

There are a surprising number of people who believe in God but do not pray very much. They say they find praying difficult. I took a short survey of the people who mentioned feeling that way, and here are some of the reasons they gave. See if you recognize yourself in any of these.

*"I find praying difficult because there are many different kinds of prayer, and I'm not sure how to pray."* It's true. There are many kinds of prayers. There is *praise and worship,* which is glorifying God. There is *confession,* where we open our hearts to God and ask Him to reveal all that is in them so He can cleanse them. There is *petition,* where we tell Him of our needs and the concerns of our heart. There is *intercession,* where we pray for others. How do we know which one to do and when to do it? What if we do the wrong thing? When we have more questions than answers about prayer, praying becomes too complex in our minds and we tend to avoid it. But God is not asking us to take a theology course before we come to Him. He simply wants us to share honestly from our heart. The right way to pray comes out of a heart that loves God and desires to communicate with Him.

*"I find praying difficult because I don't do it very well."* People are often hesitant to pray because they expect too much of themselves. They have heard the eloquence and power of the prayers of certain others, and they feel they must live up to that. They think they need to sound like the greatest preacher on earth. But God looks on our heart not our proficiency as a public speaker. Besides, nobody starts out as a powerful intercessor. We all begin with simple prayers that come from the heart. And there is nothing wrong with praying a prayer that someone else wrote, or saying a memorized prayer if it's a prayer your heart resonates to and you believe God could answer it. Just because someone else wrote the prayer doesn't mean

God will not hear it coming from you. Start with that and grow from there.

*"I find praying difficult because down deep I doubt whether prayer really works."* Many people doubt that God is actually listening when they pray. And if He *is* listening, they think, *Why would God listen to me? He is the God of the universe, and I'm just a tiny speck in comparison.* Or they may think prayer works, but just not *their* prayers. They don't understand how God has set it up. They think, *Why bother to ask?* But He has set Himself to act in *response* to our asking.

*"I find praying difficult because I feel I am not good enough to deserve an answer."* Many people feel God is not pleased with them because they have fallen short of what they should be or do. Because of their failures, or what they have *not* done, they think they are not worthy of His time. The truth is none of us is worthy. None of us have done all that we should. We have all fallen short. Only Jesus makes us worthy. Only the grace of God and the enabling power of the Holy Spirit helps us to live His way. God is loving and compassionate. He is not waiting to strike us with lightning because we didn't do everything right. He is waiting for us to come to Him and confess our sins so He can *make* everything right.

*"I find praying difficult because I see God as being distant."* People who don't really know God well think of Him as being a long way off, and they believe their prayers have to travel too far to reach Him. They envision their prayers evaporating in the air immediately after they pray them. If you feel your prayers are not powerful enough to make it up to God's ears, you are not alone. You would be surprised at how many people feel that way. But when we receive Jesus, He becomes the mediator between us and God. He has also given us the Holy

Spirit, who is now living *in* us, thereby giving us a direct line to the Lord. Our prayers don't have to travel far at all.

***"I find praying difficult because I am not sure I am praying in line with God's will."*** People often fear that if they were to ask for the wrong thing, it could mean trouble. They fear they might be punished for an inaccurately conceived prayer. Or that their prayer might be answered and produce a bad thing because they ask unwisely.

"The primary thing to understand about God's will is this—He *wills* that we should pray!" explained Pastor Jack. "We aren't called to analyze everything perfectly or pray excellently, but to bring our heart cry and limited perceptions to Him who is perfect and excellent and rest these matters with Him. We don't have to fear that inept praying may somehow sneak up on God's blind side and cause Him to inadvertently answer a prayer that doesn't serve the purposes of His will. An imperfect prayer won't cause a cosmic accident by slipping into heaven and sliding through the machinery of God's providence without His knowing. God will never find Himself awkwardly glancing toward earth and wondering, 'How did I ever let that prayer get answered?' "

No matter how experienced we are in prayer, we will never be perfect in our praying. We won't always have full understanding of the way God wants us to pray in every situation. But we don't have to know His perfect will *before* we pray. We can find it *as* we pray.

"Ask boldly. Ask largely. Ask in faith," Pastor Jack instructed us. "Ask as His child and then praise Him in the confidence He will work His will. But ask!"

The bottom line is that it's God's *will* for us to pray. We don't have to worry about whether it is His will to *answer* the way we prayed. God isn't going to be forced into answering something that is not His will. And we don't have to worry about asking for too much, because God doesn't have a limited supply of resources. He will not run out of anything. The solution to praying according to God's will is to always say, "Lord, may Your will be done in this matter."

***"I find praying difficult because it requires too much of my time to be effective."*** Often people believe that in order to be an effective praying person, they have to spend hours a day in prayer the way great prayer warriors of history have done. While it's true that the more time you spend in prayer, the more you can pray about and the more answers to prayer you will see, it doesn't mean that a quick prayer will be less likely to get answered. God hears every word we pray, especially when it is from a pure and loving heart. "The effective, fervent prayer of a righteous man avails much" (James 5:16). Every prayer counts, no matter how little time it took to pray it.

## What Makes Prayer Work?

***Prayer works because of what Jesus did.*** God created the earth, and then He created man to rule over it. Man lost his rule of the earth because of disobedience to God's laws. Satan gained control, and his goal is to destroy God's purpose for every person. God sent His Son, Jesus, to die for our sins and break the power of the enemy. In other words, Jesus took the penalty for man's disobedience, which is death, so those who believe in Him can live fruitfully on earth and spend eternity with God.

When Jesus rose from the dead, He commissioned everyone who believes in Him to *destroy* the rulership of the enemy and restore rulership to man. This is done through prayer.

When we pray we are applying Jesus' victory through the cross, taking the rule away from Satan and establishing the rule of God. In that way we stop the devil's work and establish the Lord's will. We take things that are wrong and make them right.

God doesn't want us just waiting around for Jesus to come back or for us to die and go to heaven. There are things He has for us to do in the meantime. He wants us to expose the enemy's lies and proclaim God's truth. He wants us to bring down the enemy's strongholds and set the captives free. He wants us to bring health where there is sickness, love where there is fear, forgiveness where there is condemnation, revelation where there is spiritual blindness, and wholeness where there is a shattered life. God's Word reveals that this can be accomplished when we pray.

*Prayer works because we live God's way.* In order to get our prayers answered, we need to walk in obedience to God's laws. "Whatever we ask we receive from Him, because we keep His commandments and do those things that are pleasing in His sight" (1 John 3:22). For starters, we need to love God with all our heart, soul, mind, and strength, and love others as ourselves (Mark 12:30-31). You may be thinking that this is enough to disqualify you right there. But God is merciful in this too, because we can pray about these issues as well. He will even help us to obey if we ask Him.

Remember, answers to prayer are not earned by our obedience. But our privilege to pray boldly is rooted in our relationship with Father God. And He has called us to walk as obedient children.

*Prayer works because we don't hesitate to ask.* God wants us to be bold in our asking. Being bold isn't stomping into the throne room of God and demanding what we think we deserve, but it is recognizing that God wants to do above and beyond what we think possible (Ephesians 3:20). This knowledge makes us courageous to ask God to do great things in us, through us, and around us.

Jesus said, "Which of you shall have a friend, and go to him at midnight and say to him, 'Friend, lend me three loaves; for a friend of mine has come to me on his journey, and I have nothing to set before him'; and he will answer from within and say, 'Do not trouble me; the door is now shut, and my children are with me in bed; I cannot rise and give to you'? I say to you, though he will not rise and give to him because he is his friend, yet because of his persistence he will rise and give him as many as he needs" (Luke 11:5-8). This suggests that we not only ask persistently, but boldly as well.

I once had someone tell me they prayed only about the big stuff because they didn't want to waste any of their prayers on small things, as if God only allows us a certain number of prayer requests per lifetime so we had better make our prayers count. God says we are to ask continually—to pray without ceasing. Not like a chant or saying the same thing over and over, but praying *all* the time about *everything,* knowing that God has no limits and is never too busy or preoccupied. He is always ready to hear from us. He wants us to ask because He wants to answer.

***Prayer works because God has set it up that way.*** The way God works His purposes in this world is through people who believe in Jesus. God says that if we pray, He will move on our behalf. And He will not only move, He will do what is impossible for us.

"There has long been a debate between human responsibility and divine sovereignty," explained Pastor Jack. "To some, an emphasis on the responsibility of man suggests that eternal issues are sacrificed on the altar of man's obvious imperfection. To others, an emphasis on divine sovereignty suggests a deterministic universe in which God's will irresistibly makes everything happen.

Too much of human responsibility produces an erratic world; too much of divine sovereignty, a fatalistic one."

Maybe we can't settle this issue to everyone's satisfaction, but we can at least agree that God has assigned us free will and He wants us to take charge of our part of this world in prayer. It begins in the prayer closet alone with Him.

## What Can I Do to Maintain a Daily Prayer Habit?

Because our culture idolizes the intellect, we don't often give value to prayer. We give greater value to reading and knowing the Bible intellectually. We would rather study the Bible because we can verify that we have covered a certain amount of ground. We can see what we have accomplished. But when we pray, we can't always see results right away. It's not a matter of disqualifying the importance of the intellect or our Bible study, it's a matter of our giving more time and value to prayer than we do.

I have been guilty of doing that myself, and that's why I have found it is better for me to pray first, *before* I read the Bible. When I start my devotional time by reading the Bible, I find it's hard to stop reading and allow enough time for prayer. But if I *pray* first, I will still read the Bible at some time during the day.

The day Pastor Jack spoke to us regarding his daily devotional habit, he taught us a practical way to structure our prayer time so that it would be more effective.

"Don't try to decide *how much* time you will devote to prayer or you will feel defeated if you can't live up to it," he instructed us. "It will become a task rather than a point of entry into devotional relationship with the living God. If you say you want to spend 30 minutes and you only pray for 15, you will feel like you failed. And feelings of failure are defeating in your efforts to have consistent prayer. If you don't set a time goal, it will never become a bondage to you—it will be a rejoicing to you instead."

Of course, we do need to determine what time each day we can be with God alone or the opportunity will slip through our fingers. I have found that it is best to pray in the morning when I first get up. If I don't do it then, it becomes much harder later, and I find myself struggling to have something more than a pray-and-run time. But it might be better for you at midmorning, lunchtime, sometime in the afternoon, or in the evening after dinner. I've tried having my main prayer time before I go to bed, but I am usually so tired by then that I spend a lot less time and I am not as clear thinking. Also, doing it then doesn't provide the advantage of having the day covered from the beginning. Regardless of when you do it, the point is to *allow* time for daily prayer so it bcomes a good habit.

Ask God to *help* you carve out the time you need to spend with Him. He will show you things you can eliminate from your schedule, or at least shorten to the point of giving you an extra 20 to 30 minutes. I have found that if I can get on my knees and pray *before* I do much else, then my day is not off and running without me while I am trying to catch up. Just as you would never leave the house in the morning without brushing your teeth, it should also be that you wouldn't think of starting your day without being alone with God—even if it is only for a few minutes. If you only get a short time with God in the morning and then try to fit in a more extensive time later, you have at least started the day on the right track.

It is good to have some paper and a pencil handy when coming before God so that you can write down what He speaks to your heart in your prayer time. He may remind you of something you would otherwise have forgotten. He might bring to mind something you need to do that you would not have thought of. These kinds of things make your life easier and less confusing or haphazard.

Your personal prayer time with God is the foundation for all other kinds of effective prayer. It's not that you *can't* pray with other people until you have prayed alone with God. If that were the case, most of us would not even be saved. Nor would we have experienced the healing, deliverance, or restoration we have due to the prayers of others for us. And we've all had times where the troubles in our lives were so great that we were sustained only by the prayers of others. But eventually, in order to move on in the things of God, we have to establish our own personal prayer time with the Lord.

## What Do I Do Now That I'm on My Knees?

I have found that it is much harder to stay focused in prayer when you have only a vague idea of what you are doing. If you have a plan of some sort when you pray, it helps you to get down to prayer more quickly and experience a more fruitful prayer time. Below are some steps I learned from Pastor Jack, plus what I learned through experience, that have really helped me to pray with clear purpose. They will help you get started, and you can go on from there as the Holy Spirit leads. You may even end up spending the whole time on just *one* of these steps, and that is fine. The point is to get you before the Lord, where all prayer begins.

### Step 1: Acknowledge God as your heavenly Father.

Say, *"Lord, I come before You today and thank You that You are my heavenly Father."* This establishes your relationship with God in the clearest of terms, because this is who God ultimately is to you.

### Step 2: Praise God for who He is and what He has done.

Say, *"Lord, I praise You for who You are and all that You have done."* Then praise Him for everything else that comes to your mind. Recognize how much you have to praise God for every single moment of your life.

Do you ever have days where everything seems to go wrong? Does it ever feel that your whole life is off track, or some of the things you are doing are not right on target? Does it ever seem as though you are invisible, as if no one sees or hears you when you say something? Do you feel as if you are insignificant or irrelevant? Or do you have the opposite experience where you think that everything you do attracts unwanted attention and you feel as though you stick out like a sore thumb? The way to combat all of these things is through praise and worship of God. That's right. I know it sounds as though those things don't relate, but they do. When you start your day with praise and worship and then tell God all that you are thankful for, you get the focus off of yourself and onto the Lord. Then the presence of God is welcomed into your life in a transforming way.

"Where worship takes place by people who know what they're doing and who they are approaching, you have more than merely the glib exercise of what could seem fanatical to the watcher," said Pastor Jack. "You find something that is a knowledgeable, perceptive, conscious participation with the Almighty Creator in making room for His rule and presence to invade what otherwise would be the chaotic scene of the world where we live—whether it's our home, our business, our block, our town, or our nation. Worship is the fountainhead of power."

This is something you should never forget. If you feel powerless, praise God for who He is. It's not that you will suddenly feel as though *you* are powerful, but you will immediately be aware that you have access to a source of power that is second to none. "If anyone is a worshiper of God and does His will, He hears him" (John 9:31). Those words alone should convince you.

*Step 3: Choose one of God's names, attributes, or characteristics and thank Him for being that to you.*

Say, *"Lord, I thank You that You are Almighty God. You are stronger and more powerful than anything I face or any enemy that opposes me."* Then choose another attribute of God you are especially thankful for that day. What has He been to you lately? What do you need Him to be to you today? For example, has He been your Deliverer, Counselor, Peace, Rewarder, Wisdom, Shield, Refiner, Overcomer, God who forgives, God who loves, or God who gives peace? Then praise Him for having been that to you. Do you need Him to be your Healer, Comforter, Redeemer, Forgiver, Strength, Resting Place, Provider, Light, or Refuge from the storm? Then thank Him for being *that* to you now.

"Require of yourself to go back into the *preceding* day and pick out one situation in which a specific characteristic of God was shown to you and make that a point of praise," instructed Pastor Jack. "Keep it current so you aren't always living on the basis of historic things He's done, as wonderful as they may be."

This is great advice because we often recall the greatest things God has done in our lives, which are good to remember, but forget the most recent ones, for which we also need to be grateful. We should acknowledge the Lord's hand in our lives every day, in every way we see it, because this strengthens our faith and gives us a heart full of thanksgiving and praise. There are many blessings we take for granted in our lives, and we need to praise God for them all.

*Step 4: Present your day to the Lord.*

Say, *"Lord, I present my day to You and ask You to bless it in every way."* I have found that when the first thing I do is ask the Lord to be in charge of my day and to put it in order, things go a lot smoother and there are far fewer unpleasant surprises.

Have you ever had big plans for your day and definite ideas about how it should go, and then it started getting crazy until nothing turned out the way you expected? Some of that is just part of life, but a lot of it can be alleviated by a personal and intimate time with God in the morning, setting your day before Him and putting it in His hands.

Everyone has challenges and difficulties in their lives. We all have times of worry, anxiety, loneliness, sadness, depression, despair, or pain. We all have things we're concerned about every day. But no matter what you face in your day, if you lay it all before the Lord and surrender it to Him, He will be in charge of it. Be specific about each detail, concern, event, or activity. Don't think that the details of your day are too insignificant to bring before God. If He cares about the hairs on your head enough to number them, then surely He cares about the things that fill your day.

Say, "Lord, I surrender my day to you." And then list before Him the things your day contains, or at least what you plan for it to contain. There are always things we don't expect, and sometimes we can't get everything done we would like to, but when you set your day before the Lord, you will see yourself make greater headway.

The Bible says, "In all your ways acknowledge Him, and He shall direct your paths. Do not be wise in your own eyes; fear the LORD and depart from evil" (Proverbs 3:6-7). Whenever we think we can handle our day by ourselves, we are being wise in our own eyes. And that is what going without prayer says to God. Even when we are about to do something we have done many times before, we still should ask God to help us. Just because we did it a certain way before and all went well doesn't mean we should assume everything will go smoothly now so we don't need to pray.

Tell the Lord specific ways you want Him to guide you. Say, "Lord, I lift before You the meeting I have this morning, the trip I'm going to take, the plans I must develop, the thing I need to purchase, the decisions I have to make, the talk I need to have, the bill I have to pay, the letter I must write," or whatever else is ahead of you that day. Then ask Him to order your day for you and be in charge of it. Ask Him to give you peace about it so that no matter what comes into it, whether expected or by surprise, you'll know that God is Lord over it all.

As you pray about your day, God will bring things to mind that you need to know or remember. He may make you aware of something you should do that you would not have otherwise thought about. He might open up opportunities for you that would not have happened otherwise. I found that presenting my day before the Lord in the morning keeps it from getting out of control later on. It seems to cut down on the unexpected, or at least make me better able to handle the unexpected when it happens. I could especially tell that this was true on the days I *didn't* present my day to the Lord and saw how out of control and tyrannized by the unexpected it became.

When you order your day before the Lord and put Him in charge of it, He will help you walk through it with great success.

### Step 5: Present your body to the Lord.

Say, "*Lord, I present my body to You this day as a 'living sacrifice' and ask You to help me be a good steward of this temple of Your spirit.*" When you present your body as a "living sacrifice, holy, acceptable to God" (Romans 12:1), it means you are submitting your entire being totally to Him.

It means acknowledging your dependence upon Him physically as well as spiritually and emotionally.

"If your body is presented to the Lord at the beginning of the day, you will find the spirit of the world less able to entice your body into any expression of disobedience," Pastor Jack explained. "Whether it's one end of the spectrum, such as temptation to sexual disobedience, or across the spectrum of potential verbal, visual, or attitudinal disobedience, or to the other end, such as the temptation to nutritional disobedience, presenting your body to God changes everything."

I have found that this is especially helpful when trying to take proper care of my health. It's almost as if the moment I present my body to the Lord, He shows me what I need to do or stop doing. He doesn't show me in a condemning way, but rather in a way that encourages and strengthens me. I sense greater motivation and resolve in myself, and I feel better able to make good choices throughout the day. Choices I might not otherwise have made.

### Step 6: Confess your sins before God and ask Him to help you live His way.

Say, *"Lord, search me and know my heart. Try me and know my anxieties. See if there is any wicked way in me, and lead me in the way everlasting* (Psalm 139:23-24). *Help me to live in obedience to your ways."*

We all feel terrible when we know we have disobeyed God or have not chosen His best for our lives. But Satan wants us to feel so condemned about it that we are too ashamed to come before God. He wants us to struggle with guilt to the point that we can't even pray. Yet the Lord has given us a way out of condemnation. It's called confession.

"People don't often know the difference between condemnation and conviction," said Pastor Jack. "The difference is that conviction will always drive you *to* the Lord while condemnation will drive you *from* Him. So if you feel condemned, know it is the adversary and turn to the Lord."

Nothing works in our lives when we don't live God's way, not the least of which is that our prayers are not answered. The Bible says, "Your iniquities have separated you from your God; and your sins have hidden His face from you, so that He will not hear" (Isaiah 59:2). Don't let unconfessed sin separate you from God. We all fail at times, so don't let any failure on your part hinder your prayers in any way. If you take care of this issue by yourself with God in the morning, you won't have to be dealing with it when you are trying to rest at night.

Ask God every day to keep you undeceived. And when He reveals any sin, confess it immediately so that you can be cleansed of it.

If you can't think of any sin in your life, ask God to show you whatever you need to see in that regard. All of us get things in our hearts, souls, minds, and emotions that shouldn't be there and are not God's best for our lives. Often we have sin in our hearts and lives and don't even realize it until we start paying the consequences for it. We need to keep ourselves current with those things. The Bible says, "If we say that we have no sin, we deceive ourselves, and the truth is not in us. If we confess our sins, He is faithful and just to forgive us our sins and to cleanse us from all unrighteousness" (1 John 1:8-9). It can't get any easier than that.

**Step 7. *Ask God to help you speak only words that bring life.***

Say*, "Lord, may the words of my mouth and the meditation of my heart always be acceptable in Your sight*

(Psalm 19:14). *May they bring life and truth to everyone who hears them.*" We are all capable of saying the wrong things or speaking words that can be hurtful to others, even if we don't mean any harm by them. What comes out of our mouths can cause trouble for our lives, but it doesn't have to happen.

The Bible says that "the preparations of the heart belong to man, but the answer of the tongue is from the LORD" (Proverbs 16:1). It also says that "out of the abundance of the heart the mouth speaks" (Matthew 12:34). Prepare your heart by filling it with God's Word. And ask Him to put a monitor on your mouth so that every word proceeding from your lips is loving, truthful, kind, comforting, edifying, wise, encouraging, and God-glorifying. He will do that.

### Step 8. Ask God for what you need.

Say, *"Lord, I ask You to meet all of my needs today. Specifically I ask for the following things."* Then tell the Lord whatever it is you need.

"God gives the birds what they need, and you're going to get what you need too," Pastor Jack explained. "But He still says you need to ask. In other words, the fact that God makes promises doesn't mean that they fall out of the sky. Just because God promised something doesn't mean He is obligated to do it automatically. There is a contingency that if you don't pray, you don't get it. Salvation is free, but nobody gets it who doesn't ask for it. God says not to worry about what you need, but you must obey His instructions and ask."

### Step 9. Pray for God's will in your life.

Say, *"Lord, may Your will be done in my life this day and every day."* When someone asked Pastor Jack, "How can I know the will of God?" he told them to ask for it every day. The more we ask God to keep us in His perfect will, the less chance we will end up *outside* of it.

The Lord may not show you the exact details of His will for you the moment you pray, but as you look back over a week, month, or year of your life, you will see how God led you, even when you weren't too sure you were on the right path at the time. And He did it because you submitted your life to His will every day.

### Step 10. Pray for other people.

Say, *"Lord, I pray for the following people."* Then list all who come to your mind. Start with the people closest to you, like immediate family members and close friends. Mention each one by name and bring them under the covering of God's blessings. Then pray for your church family and the people you will likely see in your day wherever you go. Ask God to show you whom you should be praying for during the day. He may suggest someone you don't even know to adopt in prayer. Pastor Jack told us, "The logical extension of your devotional time with the Lord is intercessory prayer." We will naturally turn to prayer for others when we've been alone with God.

## What if I Need More Power?

The greatest source of power is the name of Jesus. He told His disciples that they had not asked anything in His name before, but now they should ask *everything* in His name and they would receive from God. When we walk close to God and pray in Jesus' name, we too will see great power unleashed through us and amazing answers to our prayers (John 16:24-26). This places all focus on Jesus' person and what He accomplished on the cross.

"Praying in Jesus' name affirms your dependence upon who He is and what He has achieved through the cross," explained Pastor Jack. "Through the cross He broke the power of darkness so His purpose could be done. Prayer in His name is doing the same thing on behalf of other situations."

Another way to have more power and breakthrough in your prayers—especially for the tougher issues—is through fasting. Fasting and prayer brings your body into submission by informing it that it is not in charge.

"What happens when a person lets his body boss him around, whether it's sensually, sexually, or in any other dimension, is that he begins to be ruled by something other than the power by which he was created to be ruled, and that's the power of God," explained Pastor Jack. "Fasting is a way of saying, 'I'm a spirit being before I'm a physical being. I'm physical, so I need to eat, but I'm spiritual too, so I'll sometimes assert the supremacy of my spiritual allegiance beyond and before my allegiance to my body and its cry.' Fasting is an instrument that cripples the power of spiritual and evil forces in the realm of the darkness so they cannot sustain their grip on human life, minds, and circumstances."

When I fasted with Mary Anne for those three days and then was prayed for to be set free from depression, I witnessed the power of God in a way I had never imagined. I don't believe it happened randomly or by accident. I don't believe God was just having a good day and feeling benevolent toward me at that moment. God is *always* having a good day because everything about Him is good. He is always feeling benevolent because He is the God of love. But some things just don't happen unless we fast and pray. When we understand that powerful things occur in the spirit realm every time we fast and pray, it will no longer seem like merely starvation.

If you are facing what seem like insurmountable obstacles and you need more power in your prayers, don't just try to *survive* the battle when you can *win* the war through fasting and prayer.

## What Should I Do if My Prayers Are Not Answered?

There are many different reasons why our prayers are not answered. It may be that they just haven't been answered *yet,* because the timing isn't right for the answer to come. Or perhaps we have prayed something that is not God's will. Or our prayers *have* been answered, but we can't see it because they weren't answered the way we thought they would be.

Sometimes our prayers are not answered because we ask from a wrong heart. Perhaps our heart harbors unforgiveness towards someone. "If I regard iniquity in my heart, the Lord will not hear" (Psalm 66:18). Perhaps our heart is selfish or our motivation is off. "You ask and do not receive, because you ask amiss, that you may spend it on your pleasures" (James 4:3).

Jesus promised that if we will spend time with Him, learn of Him, get to know Him, be honest with Him, and acknowledge our sin against Him, then we can ask of Him whatever we want and He will answer. "If you abide in Me, and My words abide in you, you will ask what you desire, and it shall be done for you" (John 15:7). The key is wanting what *He* wants. When we do that, we end up *doing* His will and we find our prayers answered.

When I first came to know the Lord, I prayed about everything and was disappointed when all my prayers weren't answered. As I matured in the things of God, I realized that He and I are on the same side and my praying is actually working in partnership with Him to see His will done on earth. Then I became more consistent in prayer and not so disappointed if my prayers weren't answered immediately or exactly the way I prayed them. I trusted Him to answer in the time and way He chose. I concentrated on the praying instead of on the answers. It was freeing.

Once you have prayed, release your concerns. This doesn't mean you can't pray about the same thing again, but once you've finished a prayer, allow the issue to be surrendered into His hands so you can rest and be at peace. Don't worry about whether He heard you or if you did it right. Trust Him to take care of it. Learn to *partner* with God. "For the eyes of the LORD run to and fro throughout the whole earth, to show Himself strong on behalf of those whose heart is loyal to Him" (2 Chronicles 16:9). If you partner with God alone, you'll see more power in your prayers when you partner with others.

## Prayer Power

Heavenly Father, I thank You this day for who You are and all that You have done. I enter Your gates with thanksgiving and Your courts with praise (Psalm 100:4). I worship Your holy name. This is the day that You have made, and I will rejoice and be glad in it (Psalm 118:24). Thank You that You are my Savior, Healer, Redeemer, Deliverer, Provider, Counselor, and coming King. I specifically thank You that You are (name what you are most thankful for about the Lord that reflects His character).

I present my day to You and ask You to bless it in every way. I surrender all the details of it into Your hands. In everything I face today, I ask You to be with me. I trust You with all my heart, and I will not lean on my own understanding. I acknowledge You in all my ways and ask You to direct my paths (Proverbs 3:5-6). Order my day and be in charge of it. Help me to do all I need to do. Give me peace in the midst of the unexpected.

Lord, I present my body to You as a living sacrifice, holy and acceptable (Romans 12:1). Teach me how to treat it with care and be a good steward of it. Help me not to mistreat it in any way or use it improperly. Enable me to make good decisions with regard to maintaining healthful habits. Thank You that You are my healer. Specifically I pray for (<u>name any area where you need the Lord to help you or heal you</u>).

Teach me from Your Word so that I will know Your ways and walk in them. Help me to live in obedience to Your commands. I don't want anything to hinder my prayers. Show me any sin in my life so that I can confess it to You and be cleansed. Keep me undeceived in my heart and mind. Where I have sinned against You, I ask You to forgive and restore me. Specifically, I confess before You (<u>name any area where you have fallen short of God's ways for your life</u>). I repent of this and thank You that You are a God who forgives. Thank You that my sin doesn't have to separate me from You because by repenting of it and confessing it to You, I can be set free.

Show me anyone against whom I have unforgiveness, and I will confess that unforgiveness to You as sin. Specifically, I pray about my relationship with (<u>name anyone you need to forgive</u>). Create in me a clean heart and renew a right spirit within me (Psalm 51:10). Set me free so that my heart can be clean when I come before You. I don't want anything to keep me from fulfilling Your ultimate purpose for my life.

Lord, You have said that we will have to give account of every idle word in the day of judgment (Matthew 12:36). Help me to keep my tongue from evil and my lips from speaking deceit (1 Peter 3:10). Help me to speak only words that are true, noble, just, pure, lovely, of good report, virtuous, excellent, or praiseworthy (Philippians 4:8). Help me to always be able to give the reason for the hope that is within me (1 Peter 3:15). Help me to speak the truth in love (Ephesians 4:15). Fill me with Your love so that it flows from me in the words I speak.

I pray that You would bless my family and friends. Specifically, I lift up to You (<u>name family members and friends</u>). I also lift up to you my church family and people I see in my work and throughout my day (<u>name specific people who come to mind</u>). Show me anyone else You want me to pray for today.

Lord, I ask that You would meet all my needs this day. Thank You that You have provided for my needs in the past and will continue to provide for me in the future, as You have promised in Your Word. Help me to live in Your will. Thank You that Your will is not beyond knowing and that You reveal Yourself to me when I ask You to. Help me to abide in You so that I can understand Your ways and Your heart. In Jesus' name I pray.

↬ ↬ ↬

## Word Power

Ask, and it will be given to you; seek, and
you will find; knock, and it will be opened to
you. For everyone who asks receives,
and he who seeks finds, and to him who
knocks it will be opened.

MATTHEW 7:7-8

It is your Father's good pleasure to
give you the kingdom.

LUKE 12:32

If you then, being evil, know how to give good
gifts to your children, how much more will
your heavenly Father give the Holy Spirit to
those who ask Him!

LUKE 11:13

Continue earnestly in prayer, being vigilant
in it with thanksgiving.

COLOSSIANS 4:2

Seek the kingdom of God, and all these
things shall be added to you.

LUKE 12:31

# Three

# Finding a
# Partner

When I first started going to this new church, I loved everything about it except for one thing. It bothered me that at some point in every service, Pastor Jack would ask the congregation to stand up and turn to face people in front or in back of us. Then we were to form a circle by joining hands with three or four people. We had to introduce ourselves, share our prayer requests, and pray for one another. The whole process only took about five minutes, but it was the longest five minutes in my week. Having to look strangers in the eyes and share what I needed prayer for was unnerving enough, but having to *pray* for *them* was plain frightening. Especially because I wasn't sure how to pray.

## The Dreaded Prayer Circles

Pastor Jack always told us we weren't supposed to just sit and get fat on the teaching of the Word. We were supposed to be doers of the Word as well. "Let's keep moving on with the Lord," he would say as he waved his arm over the congregation, as if he were inviting us to come along with him to a new place.

"One of the hardest things about being a pastor is getting the sheep to move," Pastor Jack told me one day. "The sheep need to get up and go someplace, but sheep don't like to move, they like to eat. The problem is if the sheep keep eating in the same place and don't move, they eventually get down to just stubble."

We never tasted anything remotely close to stubble.

We all learned quickly that we were expected to grow. God accepted us the way we were, but He certainly wasn't going to leave us that way. We were going to be stretched and changed. All the time! One of the most important and profound ways we were stretched was in the area of prayer. And we got to practice, ready or not, every time we were in the prayer circles.

Pastor Jack *did* give us a way out of prayer circles by saying, "If you don't feel comfortable sharing your requests and praying, or if you have never done this before, just tell the people in your group that you want to observe."

People seldom did that, however. Most would always try to share and pray.

He also gave us guidelines concerning how we were to do it. For example, he specifically didn't want people to just turn and start praying without giving the details of their lives. He told us not to pray something abstract, like "God, You know our unspoken needs," and never share from our hearts. He instructed us to look around and see that no one was left out. If someone ended up outside of a circle, we were to open up ours and include them. If our circle got above five people, we were to divide into two groups. Then we were to pray for one another until we heard the music begin, which was our signal to finish up. As the congregation sang a worship song, the groups that had not yet finished completed their prayers.

In the beginning, I dreaded these prayer circles. But it didn't take long for me to notice how good it felt to be prayed for, so I was willing to endure those uncomfortable moments for the benefits that followed. Eventually, the prayer circles became an important part of my life, and I even began to look forward to them. I planned during the week what I would ask people to pray for me about on Sunday. Once I started seeing answers to those prayers, I was hooked. I realized it was probably the only time anyone on earth was praying for me, and if I had not told the people in my prayer circle about my prayer needs, no one would have known.

On a few very rare occasions when the prayer circles did not happen, I was actually disappointed.

As time went on, I grew more and more attached to the prayer circles. Not only were prayers being answered, but there was also a bonding that was happening between the people. I would see someone in church with whom I had prayed in the previous weeks, and I remembered their names and what their needs were.

"Did you find that job you were looking for, Bill?"

"Are things going smoother for you and your husband, Jenny?"

"Is your daughter doing better in school this week, Katie?"

"Did you get the house you were trying to buy, Frank?"

"Has that depression left like we prayed, Cindy?"

And people I had not known before meeting them in a prayer circle would also come up and ask about *me*.

"Are you feeling better this week, Stormie?"

"How is your mom? Is there any sign of improvement?"

"Did you get that job we prayed about?"

"Were you able to make your deadline?"

More and more, the faces in the prayer circles became familiar. And it wasn't just a superficial acquaintance, because we had shared something of our lives, souls, and hearts with one another. There was this personal link, and we had immediate reasons to care about each other. Even if we didn't remember specifics, we still knew we had spent those few minutes talking and praying, and that was a special thing. We witnessed it knitting us together as a people, and this became more important as the congregation grew larger. It became less and less a congregation of strangers, and more a family of prayer partners.

The church grew rapidly, with many receiving the Lord every week, and part of the reason for that was because of the love and care extended to people in those prayer circles. It was powerful, and people resonated to it.

I asked Pastor Jack if he was ever concerned that something strange might happen in a prayer circle, such as someone praying wrongly. He told me that the Lord had led him to start the prayer circles as a means of teaching people to pray, and he prayed that the guiding presence of the Holy Spirit would be in the center of every group. I know his prayers were answered because in all the years I attended there, I never heard of anything weird or strange happening in the prayer circles. And I personally had proof that the Holy Spirit attended those prayer times because of one particular incident I will never forget.

I had only been coming to church for a couple months and was, in fact, in church for the first time without my friend Terry. I was hurting terribly inside and in desperate need of prayer, so I especially looked forward to the prayer circle that morning. Having people pray for me was the best thing I had ever experienced. I could actually *feel* their prayers, and I was seeing answers to them.

That particular morning, I was more desperate than ever. I didn't understand what was happening at the time, but God was taking things out of my life that shouldn't have been there, such as jobs I had been doing and people I had spent time with. That painful and ongoing extraction made me feel as though my whole life were falling apart. I choked back tears the moment I entered the sanctuary and sensed the wonderful presence of God again.

When Pastor Jack asked for everyone to stand and turn to others for prayer, the circles quickly formed all around me, and I was left out of every one of them. I turned in each direction, but everyone had their backs to me. If I had felt better about myself and my life, I would have simply tapped someone on the shoulder and asked to be included. But I was too broken up, embarrassed, afraid, and intimidated. I had suffered with a spirit of rejection since the early days of my childhood when my abusive mother would lock me in a closet for hours as punishment, and this felt like rejection too, even though I knew no one was doing it deliberately. Plus, I hurt so much I couldn't talk without crying, and I didn't want to make a scene. People often cried in the prayer circles, but not *before* they introduced themselves.

The people in the circles around me were too concerned about the new people they were meeting and what they were going to say to notice me standing alone. So I turned back to face the front of the church, buried my face in my hands, and sobbed quietly. No one heard me because the room was noisy with people talking and praying.

Suddenly I felt a tap on my left shoulder. I looked up and saw a gentleman of about 40. He had a kind face and was dressed in a gray suit and tie.

"Can I pray for you?" he asked.

I nodded yes, and through sobs said, "My life is falling apart."

The gentleman was standing in the aisle, and I was the second person in my row from the end. There was a man between us, but he had his back toward us, so the gentleman was able to reach in and take hold of my hands without anyone noticing. He prayed a powerful and compassionate prayer with such authority and depth that I was amazed. It was insightful and strong, as if he knew a lot about me, and it made me cry all the more realizing that the Holy Spirit must have guided him to pray the way he did.

When the music began, he ended the prayer and left as quickly as he had appeared. I felt bad that I'd not had time to pray for *him,* but I immediately felt peace and hope, and I thanked God for it.

When the service was over, I looked everywhere for this kind man who prayed for me so that I could thank him. I had never seen him at the church before, but I remembered exactly what he looked like. Because of the way he was dressed and his godly manner, I was sure he must be one of the pastoral staff or an elder or usher. This was the early '70s, and everyone came to church dressed casually. The only ones who didn't were people in leadership of some kind. The congregation was relatively small at that time— only about 300 people—so it wasn't hard to find someone you were looking for. Yet I couldn't find *him.*

I thought perhaps he had left immediately after the service was over and I just missed seeing him. But when I asked the head usher about a man of his description who was ministering in the service, he said there was no one remotely fitting that description there that morning. I asked a number of other people, and they said the same thing.

I looked for him every week after that, but I never saw that man again. I always felt God must have sent him to help me in my time of great need, just as He sent angels or messengers to people in the Bible. As to who he was, only God knows. But I was sure the Holy Spirit had sent him.

Over the ensuing months after that incident, as I grew stronger in the Lord, I became less self-centered about prayer and more focused on the needs of others. I matured enough to think of the prayer circles as not just a way for *me* to be prayed for, but as a way for me to pray for someone else. Before every service I asked God to enable me to pray powerfully for whomever He would put in my circle. Because my life had been so impacted by the prayers of other people, I wanted to do the same for them. I asked Him to do a miracle through me.

"The purpose for our circles of prayer is not only to answer to need," Pastor Jack explained to us one day. "It is also to show us that Jesus wants to minister *through* us and we don't have to have a professional substitute. There's an enormous tendency in the body of Christ to depend on somebody else—especially a pastor—to be the avenue by which God will work, when it's the desire of God to work through *every* believer."

As time went on, countless stories and testimonies emerged about the life-changing influence of prayer circles. Many experienced a turning point in their lives as a result of the prayers of people they had never even met previously.

In one particular incident, a couple came to the church for the first time who had never been in a prayer circle before. It didn't make them uncomfortable because they had walked with the Lord for years. In fact they welcomed it, since the people in their circle were loving and there was a genuineness to what was happening. They were grateful for the opportunity to pray for others as well as to be prayed for concerning a great problem they were facing.

After they were finished praying, a young woman in their circle said she felt the Lord impress upon her heart certain steps they could take that would help them in their difficulty. Her words were so pointed and profound that the couple realized God was telling them the practical way they should approach their situation. When they got home they took those simple guidelines they felt the Holy Spirit had given them through this woman in their prayer circle and applied them to their problem. And it became a remarkable solution to something that had been tormenting their minds when they came to church that day.

In another example, a man in his late thirties came up to Pastor Jack and Anna's table in a restaurant one day and said he had attended Church On The Way a number of times when he had been into drugs and doing terribly. He was raised in a Christian home, but he had drifted far from the Lord. A friend from his work suggested he visit this church, and as soon as he walked through the door he felt the love of God and the love of people. He was raised with the idea that he needed to "get right with God" *before* going to church. But he realized while in church that God was reaching to accept him right where he was.

"When I entered the prayer circle," he said, "anybody there could have seen my situation wasn't that great. Anybody with any spiritual sensitivity would have known that I was not really walking with God. I had eight cents in my pocket and almost no gas in my car. That's where my life was. The people heard me when I told them I wasn't doing well and they prayed openly. Something happened that day in the prayer circle, and I felt for the first time that God had really heard my prayer. Within one week I was a changed person."

Within five years, that man had his life totally together and was being invited to speak in different schools about the dead-end street of drugs.

These kinds of things happened every week in multiplied hundreds of people. And as the church grew, eventually reaching 12,000 members, there would be thousands of people in a service, with hundreds of prayer circles going at once, and each man and woman was being ministered to personally. Not only were *our* lives being touched powerfully each time we participated, but it also gave us on-the-job training in praying for others.

I prayed in countless prayer circles for 23 years at the church before the Lord moved my family and me to Tennessee. Living there, we visited a number of different churches and even helped start a new church. While I so appreciated the wonderful preaching, teaching, and worship of these great churches, the thing I missed most were those once-dreaded prayer circles.

## The Powerful Twosome

I learned how to pray in the prayer circles at church, but it was awhile before I was bold enough to pray out loud at any other time. Of course, people had prayed *with* me or *for* me numerous times from the day I received the Lord. But *they* always initiated it. The first experience I had with actually calling someone to pray with me about a specific issue is indelibly etched in my memory. Through it I got a taste of the power of praying with just one other person. *I was, you might say, learning to think outside the circle.*

I had worked as a singer and actress on a particular TV show, and I contracted some kind of infection on my face from using TV makeup that had been contaminated by someone else's skin. Back in those days, makeup artists weren't using disposable products as they do today. They would use and reuse the same makeup brushes and sponges on everyone. I cringe to think of it now, but it was totally accepted back then. Unfortunately, this kind of thing happened far too often.

The TV show finished taping on Thursday night, and I went to the doctor first thing Friday morning. He prescribed medicine for it, but all weekend the infection kept getting worse and worse, creating deep, oozing sores on my face that burned. The more I saw it spreading, the more worried I became.

Monday morning when I woke up, it was unbearable. I had to rehearse that day and sing in a club that night, so I was going to try and cover it with makeup as best I could. But at the speed it was spreading, it would surely be impossible to cover for the TV show I had to film the following morning.

I called the church office and tried to get ahold of Mary Anne, the pastor's wife who had prayed for me concerning my depression, but she was gone. And so was everyone else. Monday was the church staff's day off, so only Carole, the receptionist, was there. I told her what was happening and why I needed prayer, and she immediately offered to pray with me over the phone right then. I gratefully said yes, and she prayed a powerful prayer, asking God to heal me completely. Then she said something I have never forgotten.

"The devil is going to tell you you're not healed," she boldly instructed me. "But don't listen to that. Just keep thanking God that He is your Healer and that He has healed you. It's going to feel like you are getting worse, but don't give in to those symptoms. Continue to praise God and speak God's promises of healing from His Word instead."

All evening at the club where I was singing, it felt as though the infection was deepening and spreading, and my face burned more and more. I had covered my skin with thick makeup and hoped that because the club was dimly lit, no one could clearly see my face. But on a break, in the glaring lights of the ladies' room, I glanced in a mirror and could tell it was worse. I quickly closed my eyes and thanked God for my healing, just as Carole had instructed me to. I told Satan I wasn't going to listen to any of his lies about me getting worse because I was healed by the power of God. I quoted all the Scriptures I had written down about healing.

On the way home, I did the same thing, only this time I shouted God's Word out loud in the car. "Thank You, Lord, that You were wounded for my transgressions and bruised for my iniquities. Thank You that by Your stripes I am healed (Isaiah 53:5). Thank You that because I fear Your name, the Sun of Righteousness shall arise with healing in His wings for me (Malachi 4:2). Thank You that You forgive all my iniquities and heal all my diseases" (Psalm 103:3).

That night, after I went to bed, I still felt the infection getting worse. Whenever I woke up in the night, I praised God for His healing and again quoted from the Scriptures. It was a tremendous battle, but I refused to give place to my fears. When I awoke the next morning, I immediately ran to the mirror and could not believe my eyes. The open sores had closed completely and receded to the point that all I could see of them were pink spots where they had been. It was miraculous. I had never witnessed anything disappear so fast and so completely. I was easily able to cover my skin with makeup for the TV show that day, and that was the end of it.

Could that have been just a coincidence? If it was, it's interesting that these kinds of coincidences only happened when I prayed. The healing astounded me, and because of it my faith increased and I became a believer in the power that comes from praying together.

## The Significant Others

One of the things that happens when we are filled with the Holy Spirit and pray for others is the Holy Spirit *in* us moves *through* us to touch the people we are praying for. The Holy Spirit is called the Comforter because He comes *alongside* people to bring comfort. When we are filled with the Holy Spirit, we too have the ability to come alongside the people to comfort them and build them up. In doing that, we confirm their significance to God and to us.

"Come *alongside* of people, don't come *at* them," Pastor Jack always instructed us. "Be comforting and not preachy. It helps to remember that the word for 'comfort' in Greek is *paraklesis*, which means to come alongside because you're invited. There is a tendency with some people who try to minister to a person who has a need to come *at* them in a way that makes it difficult for the other person to receive. It's something of the tone of voice, something of the style that comes as a result of trying to mirror what they've seen platformed in church Christianity. It's not that what was platformed is wrong, but it's that you can't operate from a platform. In our daily life, we're *alongside* people."

One time I was in a prayer circle of five people, and a man in his late fifties, who seemed very beaten down and sad, requested prayer for himself. He had been unemployed for a long time and wanted to find work. Another young man in the circle insensitively and almost arrogantly said, "Your problem is that you don't have enough faith. I'm going to pray for you to have more faith!"

I felt sad for the poor man who was out of work, because I could see that what the young man said, and the way he said it, made him feel worse. I was too new in the Lord to be courageous enough to come to his defense, but fortunately there was another elderly and seasoned gentleman to my left who spoke up and said, "We all need more faith. There is no one here who doesn't. We also all go through difficult times, and that doesn't mean we don't have faith. It means we need our brothers and sisters in the Lord to come alongside of us in prayer. Let's pray for our brother here to find a job."

That man's compassionate prayer impressed me deeply because I could sense the love and mercy of God in it. And I saw how it touched the man who had asked for prayer. His face and demeanor reflected encouragement and hope after we finished praying.

How we relate to others around us is extremely important. The words "one another" are mentioned many times in the Bible, and each time they are, it is clear that we are to treat others as if they are significant and valuable. Below are just a few of the things God says we should do for one another. Can you see, as you read each one, how you might be able to accomplish these to some degree in prayer?

## Fifteen Things We Should Always Do for One Another

| | |
|---|---|
| Mourn with one another | Ezekiel 24:23 |
| Have peace with one another | Mark 9:50 |
| Be affectionate to one another | Romans 12:10 |
| Be like-minded toward one another | Romans 15:5 |
| Receive one another | Romans 15:7 |
| Care for one another | 1 Corinthians 12:25 |
| Serve one another | Galatians 5:13 |
| Bear with one another | Ephesians 4:2 |
| Be kind and forgive one another | Ephesians 4:32 |
| Submit to one another | Ephesians 5:21 |
| Comfort and edify one another | 1 Thessalonians 5:11 |
| Consider one another | Hebrews 10:24 |
| Love one another | 1 Peter 1:22 |
| Have compassion for one another | 1 Peter 3:8 |
| Minister your gifts to one another | 1 Peter 4:10 |

The one that is mentioned by far the most frequently in the Bible is to "love one another." The Bible instructs us to "put on love, which is the bond of perfection" (Colossians 3:14). We are perfected in the Lord when we come alongside others with love and pray for them.

The Bible also mentions many things we are *not* to do to one another, because doing these things to other people hurts them and trivializes their existence. Below are just a few. Can you see, as you read each one, how praying for others could keep you *from* doing these things?

## Ten Things We Should Never Do to One Another

| | |
|---|---|
| Don't lie to one another | Leviticus 19:11 |
| Don't oppress one another | Leviticus 25:14,17 |
| Don't rule over one another | Leviticus 25:46 |
| Don't grumble against one another | James 5:9 |
| Don't betray or hate one another | Matthew 24:10 |
| Don't wrong one another | Acts 7:26 |
| Don't burn in lust for one another | Romans 1:27 |
| Don't judge one another | Romans 14:13 |
| Don't push one another | Joel 2:8 |
| Don't go to law against one another | 1 Corinthians 6:7 |

We don't have to look far in order to find people who are hurting because of something someone has done to them. But God wants to comfort them through our prayers. He wants to change their lives and bless them with His purposes for them. He asks us to proclaim the significance of others by joining in prayer with them.

## The Indispensable Prayer Partners

After I experienced that amazing healing, I began to think, *Wouldn't it be great to have a prayer partner I could call to pray with whenever I needed prayer?*

"Who could I pray with on a regular basis, Lord?" I asked.

Immediately a young woman came to mind. Diane had been my closest friend for years, but we had become distant. We had been into the occult together and were always in unity about spiritual things, so when I received the Lord and stopped all occult practices, she felt that I'd not only lost my mind but had deserted her as well. I had been praying for her to be open to the Lord, and in fact prayed for her often in the prayer circles at church, but she was solidly resistant.

I prayed about her as a possible prayer partner, and later that day I called to see how she was doing. I had not spoken to her in weeks, and so I was surprised to find her in an extremely desperate state. She told me she had been severely depressed for some time and was agoraphobic. That meant she was afraid to go out of her house and be with people in public places. In fact, she was having panic attacks when she went to the grocery store. I couldn't believe how rapidly she had gone downhill since I last spoke with her.

Diane and I had been best friends in high school because we shared a deep understanding of one another's emotional pain. She had been raised by an alcoholic mother, and what she remembered most from her childhood was coming home from school every day to find her mother passed out drunk on the living room floor. Like me, she always struggled to keep her home life a secret and maintain a good façade for other people.

On that particular day when I called, Diane was surprisingly open to everything I had to say about the Lord. I knew it was an answer to prayer. She said she had observed a remarkable difference in me and wanted what I had found. In my own awkward and inexperienced way, I led her to the Lord over the phone. I invited her to come to church with me the following Sunday, and she accepted.

Diane lived a long way from me in the opposite direction of the church, so I didn't pick her up on Sunday. I worried about whether she would actually make it there, but I prayed with her over the phone Saturday night that she would be strong and not allow fear to control her life. I reminded her that she had Jesus living in her heart now, giving her a source of strength with which to resist and rise above those fears. How overjoyed I was when I saw her pull into the parking lot of the church on Sunday, just in time for the service.

In the sanctuary she sat between me and Michael so she would feel safely surrounded, and she cried through the entire service just the way I did. When Pastor Jack gave his touching and compelling talk asking people to come to the Lord, she lifted her hand to receive Jesus. Again! I was thrilled because I wasn't sure I had done it right anyway. Also, it was a confirmation that she was serious about this step and not just doing it for me.

God not only heard my prayers for Diane's salvation, but also for a prayer partner. After she received the Lord, we started praying together regularly over the phone at least three times a week. Through the next few years, we saw our prayer times become instrumental in each of us finding the healing and wholeness God had for our lives. From that time on, having a prayer partner became an indispensable necessity I could not afford to be without.

If you never had someone praying with you when you were growing up, you are not alone. I didn't have that either. If you don't have someone praying with you regularly now, don't worry, because you can pray that God will bring one or more prayer partners into your life. Ask God to send you someone with whom you can agree on a regular basis. Someone with whom you can be mutually accountable in prayer. It could be someone you already know, such as a friend, roommate, or family member. Or someone in your neighborhood, in a class you are taking, or at work. It could even be someone new He brings into your life specifically for that purpose. Someone you may have seen but never thought about in that regard. He will show you who it is.

One word of caution. When you approach a person to ask if they want to be your prayer partner for a season, don't be upset or feel rejected if they turn you down. That just means they are not the right person for *you,* or the timing isn't right for *them.* I asked my husband if he wanted to be my regular prayer partner, but he wasn't interested in a set schedule. He just wanted to pray when he felt like it, but that wasn't enough for me. He likes to pray for the big picture; I like to pray for the details. Though we pray together often, I have prayer partners to pray with me regularly. Don't become discouraged if it takes awhile to find the right person. Give God time.

When you ask a person to pray with you, don't be afraid to share any fears you have about praying. Tell them if you are afraid you won't know what to say, or that you won't have enough faith, or whatever else concerns you. For example, when I first started to pray with other people, I was afraid God would not answer my prayers, as if all answers to prayer depended entirely on me. I also felt reticent to pray in front of others who had a better command of the language or a greater knowledge of *how* to pray. I finally came to understand that God wasn't looking for eloquence, just a faithful and pure heart. Once I realized that *my* job was to pray, and it was *God's* job to answer, I felt more at ease. It wasn't all up to me. It was up to God. All I had to do was have faith that God answers prayer.

When you start praying regularly with a partner, you will see great things happen. That's because each of you brings the Holy Spirit in you, and that power increases exponentially. Also, your faith will inspire growth in the other person's faith, and their faith will increase yours. That produces a snowball effect which enables you to believe for bigger and better things. Once you have a prayer partner, you will see God move with power in your life and you will never want to be without one.

## The Necessary Honesty

One of the most important things I learned about joining in prayer with another person was the need for honesty. Too often we are less than forthcoming when we share our prayer requests with another person, but honesty before both God and man is crucial. I have seen many marriages where a husband or wife would rather risk divorce than let someone know they had a problem and ask for prayer. Or if they did ask for prayer, they weren't honest about the seriousness of their situation. They believed their struggle was so private that they couldn't call someone to come alongside and help bear the burden of it in prayer.

Often people don't ask for help because they are embarrassed to admit they need it. Or they don't want to bother anyone with their problems. But there are people God has *called* to come alongside us in prayer. If we don't give them the opportunity, because either we don't ask or we don't share honestly, then we forfeit many of the blessings God has for us.

Prayer is one of the most important ways in which we can "bear one another's burdens" (Galatians 6:2). You might not be able to bear someone's financial burden or the burden of their poor health, unhappy marriage, or problem child, but you can pray for them to have provision, be healed, find restoration, or defeat a rebellious spirit.

Some people say that you should *never* speak things that are negative. This is the way my occult practices were. That kind of thinking brought me to the brink of suicide, because I could never face the truth. I couldn't share what was *really* happening with anyone and ask for help. I found after I came to the Lord that there were even Christians who believe that too. They say that you should never confess negative things. If that's true, then how do you ever ask for help? I'm not talking about complaining and always speaking negatively about something, I'm talking about sharing your pain and need honestly with people so that they know how to pray for you. I'm talking about walking in the light of the Lord together with other believers so you can be cleansed from all the effects of sin in your life—yours and that of the world around you (1 John 1:7).

"An honest and forthright disclosure is an important feature of our understanding the believing life," said Pastor Jack. "There is something about walking in the light of transparent relationship that advances the purifying work of God's grace in our lives. The reason it's important is because some people suggest that if you are forthright in describing your pain, your problem, your difficulty, or your struggle, then you are poor-mouthing what God has done for you and negating the functioning of vital faith. That isn't biblical. Otherwise you would not find the apostle Paul saying, 'I asked God three times for an answer to my problem and it didn't go away.' There are some people who would fault Paul. They say he should only have said it just one time and then praised God and confessed the victory. Paul kept asking and asking and finally, when nothing happened, the Lord spoke to him and said, 'Paul, My strength is made perfect in weakness and My grace is sufficient for you.' He learned a dimension of grace during that time that he wouldn't have learned any other way. A forthright disclosure is not a violation of the principle of faith."

Paul was the same man who said, "I can do all things through Christ who strengthens me" (Philippians 4:13), and "in all these things we are more than conquerors through Him who loved us" (Romans 8:37). Yet he also said, "Our bodies had no rest, but we were troubled on every side. Outside were conflicts, inside were fears" (2 Corinthians 7:5). Paul knew the victorious life in Jesus, but he was fully honest in telling how things were. He had seen answers to prayer, but he wanted to explain how it was. One of the most important aspects of praying together with another person is being able to open our heart honestly and tell it like it is.

I have found that in the prayer groups I have had—and I have always had one going on for the past 30 years—the people who would open up and share honestly were the ones who saw the greatest answers to their prayers. They progressed faster in their walk with God. They saw great breakthrough where others, who would not share as honestly, did not. It really comes down to being honest before *God* about our needs. Yes, He already knows them, but He still wants us to ask.

Of course, sharing honestly is always a risk, and in the end you have to decide if you are willing to take it. That's why finding trustworthy people to be your prayer partners is important. When my husband and I were having problems, I decided I was willing to risk having the whole world know about them if someone chose to spread the word. So I spoke honestly to my prayer partners, whom I trusted, and prayed that no one would breach my trust by revealing this confidential information to other people. Thankfully, I had trusted in mature and sensitive believers, and no one ever gossiped about our struggle.

It's not a shame to have problems, but it is certainly a shame to end up in trouble because of being too embarrassed or prideful to ask for help. Let's be honest. It's the best policy.

## The Golden Opportunities

Diane was my prayer partner for a few precious years until she developed breast cancer and became very ill. We prayed together as long as we could, and then it became impossible for her. When she died I missed her terribly, not only as a friend and sister in the Lord, but also as a prayer partner. I asked God to send me another prayer partner who would be willing to pray as often and as faithfully as we did.

It took awhile to find someone, but in the interim I learned to take advantage of every opportunity I could to pray with another person. I was so desperate for prayer that I would grab anyone's hand who was willing and pray with them. If I had a prayer need, I didn't rest until I found someone who would pray with me about it. The more I did that, the more I became aware of all the golden opportunities there are around us to pray with another person. Prayer partners are everywhere if we will just open our eyes to see them. Many people are longing to pray with someone but are reticent, for one reason or another, to ask.

"The idea of intercession, as it occurs in the Scriptures, recognizes a chance element," said Pastor Jack. "One meaning of the word used for *intercession* means *to happen* or *to light upon by chance*. God has people in different places at different times, and they often don't realize they are there specifically for that moment and time. A prayer circumstance can arise that is a divinely appointed place for the lightning of heaven to strike, but it's waiting for a point of contact on earth to draw on the power. Some people say that if God could arrange for a person to be at a certain place to pray, why didn't He just go ahead and arrange the answer to the prayer. But He doesn't work that way. He desires that our prayers *partner* with His power. We are the lightning rod of earth. God *could* 'strike'—or manifest His mightiness—without us, but He does not act randomly. Rather, in His sovereign will, He has chosen to work on earth through partnership with those who want and welcome His will."

We may think that the things that happen to us are all by chance, but they are not. We may think, *Isn't it interesting that I happened to be there at the moment this person needed prayer,* but it's not just interesting, it was divinely arranged. There are people everywhere who will pray with you on the spur of the moment, and you need to recognize these golden opportunities and not let them pass by.

When I learned to pray with a prayer partner about the things that concerned me, I found myself praying more and with greater direction and purpose. As a result, things really started to progress in my life. I experienced more deliverance, healing, growth, and success. And I came to see that these things happened not only because I was being prayed for, but also because I was praying for others. Your prayer for another person will benefit *you* as much as it does them. And their prayer for you will bless *them* as much as it does you.

God has someone with whom He wants you to pray. Don't hesitate to ask Him who that might be. You may be pleasantly surprised.

## Prayer Power

Lord, You have said that when just two people are gathered in Your name, You are there in the midst of them (Matthew 18:20). What a wonderful promise to us. You have also said that when two of us *agree* in prayer, You will answer (Matthew 18:19). I pray You will help me to find someone with whom I can agree. I ask that You would specifically send one or more persons into my life who are willing to pray with me on a regular basis. Let them be people who are trustworthy and mature in Your ways, and who have faith to believe for answers to prayer. Help me be sensitive as to whom they might be.

If I approach a person and ask them to pray with me, help me not to be hurt or offended if they refuse. Help me to be big enough to recognize that perhaps they were not the right person for that moment. Keep me from giving up and shrinking back from asking for prayer. Help me to pay attention to what *You* want instead of what *others* are thinking.

Teach me how to be a strong prayer support for others. Work through me when I pray with another person so that I will pray right on target. Help me to hear Your Holy Spirit leading me and giving me knowledge, revelation, and discernment. Show me things I would not be able to see on my own. Make me into a powerful prayer warrior. Do miracles through me when I pray.

Give me boldness to *ask* for prayer from others. Help me to be honest in sharing my requests so that the issues are faced and problems are solved because we are able to pray in accordance with the truth. I don't want to conceal things out of pride or fear that need to be revealed. I don't want to give a wrong picture about my situation in order to impress others. Help me to be fully transparent so that prayers for me can be fully powerful.

Help me to recognize opportunities to pray with others that I might not otherwise have seen. Give me courage to pray for people so that I will not hesitate or hide from opportunities that present themselves. Enable me to be more conscious of how I obey Your leading than how I appear to others. Help me to come alongside people in prayer just like You, Holy Spirit, come alongside of me. Help me to comfort others the way You always bring comfort to me.

Lord, grow me up in knowledge of the power of prayer. As I reach out to pray with and for others, give me ever-increasing faith to believe for the answers. I know that with You, God, nothing is impossible. Help me to trust Your willingness to hear and respond. Enable me to pray according to Your will at all times. My ultimate prayer is for Your will to be done in all things. In Jesus' name I pray.

∽ ∽ ∽

## Word Power

If two of you agree on earth concerning
anything that they ask, it will be done for them
by My Father in heaven.

MATTHEW 18:19

Bear one another's burdens, and so
fulfill the law of Christ.

GALATIANS 6:2

Rejoice always, pray without ceasing,
in everything give thanks; for this is the will of
God in Christ Jesus for you.

1 THESSALONIANS 5:16-18

Whatever things you ask in prayer,
believing, you will receive.

MATTHEW 21:22

Be anxious for nothing, but in everything
by prayer and supplication,
with thanksgiving, let your requests be made
known to God; and the peace of God, which
surpasses all understanding, will guard your
hearts and minds through Christ Jesus.

PHILIPPIANS 4:6-7

# Four

# Join the Group

Our church had been growing at a rapid rate when Pastor Jack asked Michael and me to be one of the married couples taking classes in preparation to lead a home group. After we were ready, we opened our home to what would become the experience upon which my future would eventually be built. It ultimately led to the writing of all my books, especially those on the power of prayer. Let me explain how that happened.

Before the first meeting we led in our home, I felt great excitement and anticipation. I already had a tremendous love for the people—sight unseen—because of all the prayer that had gone into preparing for that day. It was a sensation I had never experienced before, because I didn't understand how you could love people you didn't even know. But God gives you *His* heart for people when you pray for them, and Michael and I had been praying for months.

We had no idea who would show up—if anyone—because people chose a site according to location. Addresses were listed in a bulletin at church, and people went to the one most convenient for them. As it turned out, 18 people came, which was plenty for a home group.

It was like Christmas morning, because each one who came was a special gift to us.

According to the guidelines Pastor Jack had given us, Michael took charge of the worship time, read from the Scriptures, and gave a very short teaching from that Bible passage. Then everyone shared how the Scripture and teaching spoke to their lives. All of that took about 45 minutes, after which Michael turned the meeting over to me, and then I led the prayer time that followed. When I asked if anyone had a prayer request, the response was overwhelming. It was immediately evident that there were far more prayer needs than we had time to adequately pray for that day.

We struggled through the first few meetings trying to fit everything into the time allotted, and then it became apparent that in addition to this once-a-month meeting, we needed to have another time when we could come together without children and concentrate on prayer alone. So we scheduled a prayer meeting for the first Friday night of every month, and again the response was overwhelming. Everyone showed up.

I realized at this Friday night prayer meeting that we needed to separate the group by gender or we would end up going way too late. Besides, I suspected there were needs in the women that were not being addressed in the mixed group. So the men stayed in the living room with Michael, and I took the women into our bedroom. I felt the women needed that privacy in order to share openly.

We didn't have nearly enough chairs, so the eight women and I took off our shoes and sat in a circle on our king-size bed. When I asked for a volunteer to go first, a young woman, whom I will call Kelly, raised her hand. She was a gentle and naturally pretty girl in her late twenties who always came with her husband and two young children.

"Tell us how you want us to pray for you, Kelly," I said.

"I hate my life and I don't know what to do about it," Kelly said, bursting into tears and then convulsive sobs.

Her statement jolted me and, although I didn't look to see anyone else's reaction, I'm sure it affected everyone in the room the same way. I wasn't shocked at someone hating their life. I wasn't even shocked at someone breaking down and sobbing about it. I had been there and done that. I knew what it felt like. But I was shocked that *she* was saying it. Kelly and her husband were an unusually uplifting and godly couple with wonderful children. The kind of family everyone loved and admired. She appeared to be the perfect wife and mother, someone who was always together and overflowing with kindness.

I wanted to drop my jaw and say, "You've got to be kidding!" in response. But I didn't because I was the leader. Instead I maintained a calm assurance that this was no abnormal request. And I'm glad I did, because hers was only the first of many to come.

Kelly's revelation was an eye-opening experience. It showed how much hurt there can be in people we don't suspect have any. Only God knows how many people keep themselves together with merely a thin glue of desperation in order to survive. Even good *Christian* people.

Kelly went on to explain how nothing in her life had turned out the way she thought it would. It wasn't that she had a bad marriage, but it didn't meet all of her needs. Plus she had such high expectations of herself as a wife, mother, and servant of the Lord that she constantly felt like a failure and easily became depleted physically and emotionally. In questioning her to see where this was coming from, I felt led by the Holy Spirit to ask her if she had been denying an important part of who she was in order to try and be all things to all people.

She started to sob again and said, "Yes, I have. As far back as I can remember I have wanted to be a writer. But after I got married and had children, I haven't been able to do any writing at all."

"Kelly, we are going to pray for you to be released from the sadness and hopelessness you feel about your life," I told her. "This discouragement is the devil's plan for you. But God has another plan, and it doesn't have to do with you meeting other people's expectations. It has to do with you putting all your expectations in the Lord. God doesn't want you to feel the way you do, but He understands it and has an answer for your pain. He has given you gifts that are to be used for His glory, and you will always feel frustrated if you are not using them. If God has put writing in your heart, then you should be doing that a little every day. You don't have to neglect the rest of your life in order to do this. Just get a special notebook for that purpose and write something of what God puts on your heart in it."

The seven other women agreed with that, and we all laid our hands on Kelly and prayed for her as the Spirit led us. It was a powerful prayer time, and she sobbed through it all. We broke the grip of despair and hopelessness that held Kelly captive, and afterward the sense of relief and release was clearly visible on her face.

The following month, Kelly came back to the prayer meeting and shared what had happened since the night we all prayed for her. She had bought a journal and started writing every day as I suggested, and she was sensing new vision for her life and hope about her future. She also felt greater peace and fulfillment. Through the following months, we continued to pray about different aspects of this issue every time we met for prayer, and she began to blossom.

Kelly wasn't the only one who had deep needs. Every woman in the group shared a heartfelt story, and one by one we saw miraculous answers to countless prayers. Maybe it was because we sat in a circle so informally that made each woman feel comfortable enough to be gut-wrenchingly transparent about what was going on in her life. Or perhaps it was because we had been brought together by God specifically for that purpose. I think it was a combination of both. I have since learned that you can't find the full extent of your true destiny and purpose apart from other believers who stand with you in prayer.

## Who Benefits from a Home-Based Prayer Group

Our home group eventually grew to 75 members, which was not only too crowded for our house at the time, but overwhelming in terms of meeting the tremendous needs of the people. It was the size of a small church, only Michael and I weren't full-time pastors. We had full-time jobs in addition to our ministry. We led the group for well over a year before it was divided and other leaders were trained to take portions of the group into their own homes. By that time, we were ready for a rest.

On the last meeting of our group, everyone gave testimony to the many answers to prayer we had seen in the time we were together. It was breathtaking to hear the stories, and the flow of tears and praise couldn't be contained. What began as a handful of strangers—whose common bond was their church, their pastor, and their love of the Lord—ended as a spiritual family with deep connections and memories that would be with us for a lifetime.

In that time, we had seen answers to all but one of the major prayer requests. That was from a young woman I will call Jennifer. She had not received an answer to her persistent request that she be able to have a baby. Every time our group met, we prayed for Jennifer to either get pregnant or be able to adopt a child. We prayed her through each test and possible medical solution, and every application to an adoption agency, but there was never any breakthrough. At our last meeting, we felt sad that this prayer had not been answered—especially with everyone sharing the glorious answers to *their* prayers.

I didn't see Jennifer for a while after that because the church had grown so large and we now had multiple services. She and her husband attended a different service than we did. Well over two years later, I received a phone call from her telling me that she and her husband were finally able to adopt a baby boy. I was thrilled beyond words.

"God, You are so good. Thank You for answering that prayer," I said.

Jennifer and her husband moved away not long after that. But several years later she called again to let me know that she had become pregnant and given birth to a baby boy. Somewhere in the world those boys have over 70 spiritual aunts and uncles who are grateful that God is faithful to answer prayer. That delayed answer taught us all that God's timing is perfect and we must be faithful to continue in prayer and not grow weary in waiting.

Leading that home group became just as rewarding and life-changing as it was challenging. Some of the most memorable, positive, and tender times of my Christian walk were as a result of being home group leaders. It grew us up in the things of the Lord far more quickly than we would have otherwise. Knowing that 73 people were looking to us for help in so many crucial areas kept Michael and me on our knees and solidly grounded in the things of God. We were always acutely aware that without God's enabling power and grace we couldn't do it.

As to who benefits from a home-based prayer group, the answer is everyone. These kinds of groups afford us the opportunity to feel intimately connected to people who love the Lord and believe the same way we do. They give us faith-filled people to turn to in a time of need. They make us feel loved and supported, and provide us the opportunity to share the love of God with others on a regular basis. Getting to know people through the prayer requests they share forms a bond between you that will never be broken.

## Where Two or More Are Gathered

After our home group ended, we became members of home groups led by other people. They were great, but they didn't have the extended prayer times we'd had, and I missed that so much. So I contacted five other women and organized a prayer group by mail. Because we all lived far from each other and had babies, no one had the time to come to my house and pray for three hours while juggling children.

The way it worked was once a month I sent my prayer requests to the five women and included a blank letter with a stamped envelope. They filled out their requests on the letter and sent it back. Then I made copies of their requests and mailed them to all the other ladies. We committed to praying for each other throughout the month, which meant on any given day there was at least one or more people praying for us. Although it was labor intensive for me, this worked well for a while.

Looking back now, that method seems almost primitive, though at the time it was innovative. We benefited from praying for each other, but it was a prayer group that never got together. I missed the personal contact. I could always feel the power of God move when praying with other people, and I wanted to do that again on a regular basis. We did have a group of people who met in our house for prayer once a month, but this was an affinity group, which meant everyone in the group had the same type of occupation. (More about that later in this chapter.) Once a month wasn't enough for me.

When my family and I were able to move closer to the church and my children were both in school, God spoke to my heart clearly that I was supposed to organize a weekly prayer group of women in my home. I had started writing books and doing some speaking, and I knew I could not maintain any kind of public ministry without the support of such a prayer group behind me. I was nervous about asking people because I wasn't sure if anyone would be interested in coming. I should have known that if God calls you to do something, He is faithful to provide what or who is needed to make it happen.

I prayed about this group for nearly two months before asking anyone to join because I didn't want to make a mistake. I knew from experience when my husband and I led the home group that you don't really know someone until you are in a prayer group with them. The true character of each person surfaces when the walls come down and the truth comes out. That's why there should be a certain level of compatibility and trust among the members of a regular weekly prayer group. It is of utmost importance that no one in the group violate the confidential aspect of sharing requests. If someone is repeating to other people what a person shares in confidence, or if there is someone in the group who is upsetting to the rest, people will dread coming and eventually stop.

As I prayed about the different women God put on my heart, I waited until I had peace about one before I asked her. I knew I would not have the courage to ask these women if I wasn't certain that God had clearly instructed me to do so. I asked each woman to commit for one year, which was enough time to get something accomplished by pressing through in prayer on issues and giving God time to answer. It also gave a cutoff time for anyone who needed to leave the group for whatever reason. They could make a change without feeling awkward or uncomfortable.

God brought the perfect women to be part of this group. As in our original Friday night prayer times, the members of this group had heartrending needs as well. They were women who were deeply committed to God, full of faith, grounded in the Word, and whose lives were in order, yet they had struggles with marriage, children, health, emotions, work, and finances like everybody else. They each had a past they wanted to get free of and a future they wanted to move into. As we went through this journey of faithfully praying every week, we saw God answer prayer after prayer after prayer. And each of our lives was changed.

At the end of each year, I asked the women to pray about whether they were going to be in the group the following year. Few people ever dropped out, but if anyone did, I asked the Lord to show me whom I should ask to replace her. When God showed me someone, I would first ask the rest of the group to pray about her as well. If we all had peace, then I would ask her.

In the past 20 years, I have always had a prayer group in my home. The faces have changed many times because people moved away or *I* moved away, but the effect has always been dynamic no matter who was in it. I know I could not have written the books I have, nor would they have gone all over the world and been translated into 15 languages, if it weren't for the prayers of my prayer partners. God has done amazing things in answer to the prayers of faithful people.

## Why We Find Strength in Unity

When Pastor Jack was a young teenager, he heard a missionary lady tell how she was trapped with some people in a dry riverbed just as a flash flood came. The people immediately joined hands and withstood that danger by strengthening each other. As they united against the sweeping waters, their lives were spared.

That is exactly what a prayer group does. People join together to stand strong against things that would seek to wash away their lives and destroy them. The Bible says that rather than be anxious about our lives, we are to pray about them (Philippians 4:6-7). And when we find ourselves in serious circumstances, we are to stand united with other believers and pray for one another.

One of the first things I learned in leading prayer groups was the need for unity. Jesus said that "if two of you agree on earth concerning anything that they ask, it will be done for them by My Father in heaven" (Matthew 18:19). That word *agree* is very important. The Greek word for unity is *sumphoneo*. It's where we get the word "symphony." In order to have harmony, there are a number of things we need to agree on.

First of all, we need to agree on the basics, such as Jesus is "the way, the truth, and the life" and "no one comes to the Father except through" Him (John 14:6). We must also agree that the Bible is inerrant and inspired by God, that Jesus was born of a virgin and lived a sinless life, that He died for our sins and rose from the dead, and that whoever believes in Him will have everlasting life.

"These are the essential elements of our God-given covenant, which are our grounds for prayer," said Pastor Jack. "They are God's word of sure promise, God's Son of sovereign power, and salvation's provision. Belief in these things must happen in order to come together in unity."

We don't have to agree on every minute detail of our beliefs, but it is crucial that we agree on certain foundational truths, otherwise we are not standing on the same foundation. "Can two walk together, unless they are agreed?" (Amos 3:3). The answer is "No." We have to agree on *who* it is exactly that we are praying to, and that His Word not only invites our prayers, but it also promises answers.

Then, it's very important that we agree on *what* we are praying about. God wants us to "be of the same mind toward one another" with regard to that (Romans 12:16). I found that one of the hardest things in leading a prayer group was getting people to formulate their requests clearly and align them with God's will. When someone's requests were vague, uncertain, or a little off base, the other people did not know how to pray.

For example, two sisters were praying about their elderly father, who was suffering with a painful and terminal illness. One wanted to pray for his complete healing while the other wanted to pray that he be released to be with the Lord and not suffer any more. With each of them praying for different things, they were unable to come to a point of unity. But then they prayed, "Lord, may Your perfect will be done in my father's life. If Your will is to heal him, heal him completely and take away all pain and suffering. If Your will is to take him to be with You, take away all misery and give him Your peace and a deep sense of Your presence."

It's important to first determine exactly *how* you want to pray so that the group can be in unity.

In the couples group my husband and I led, a young actor, whom I will call Jason, asked our group to pray that he would get a particular part in a huge stage play opening in Los Angeles. He had auditioned for it, and after a number of callbacks, was one of two finalists called to audition one last time. He asked the group to pray that he would get the part. What we actually prayed was that he would get the part *if* it *was God's will*. But if it *wasn't,* that God would bring something even better into his life.

I don't think Jason heard the *God's will* part of the prayer, however, because when he did not get the part he became bitter about it. He got mad at God and left the church, the prayer group, and eventually his wife. Obviously, his walk with God was not built on a strong foundation, and that's probably one of the reasons God did not answer that prayer the way Jason wanted Him to. God gives us certain blessings only when our hearts are right and we are ready to handle them in the proper way.

The mistake we made as leaders was in allowing the group to pray without first bringing *him* into agreement with us. Jason needed to agree that the most important thing was for God's will to be done. God invites us to ask for the desires of our heart, but those desires must not be in conflict with the desires of *His* heart and *His* will for our lives. If they are, we have to let them go. God's will must be the ultimate desire of our heart in all that we do.

If I could do it all over again, I would say to Jason, "God loves you so much that He wants the best for you. But He does things in our lives *His* way, and He wants to know that we love Him enough to submit to His will. When we ask for the desire of our heart, we must above all ask for the desires of *God's* heart to be done. And we have to be prepared for either a yes or a no answer and trust that whichever it is, it's God's will for our life. If the answer is 'no' to something we want, it's because God has something better for us."

After that, whenever someone in one of my prayer groups shares about their situation without clearly stating what their request is, I ask them, "How do you want us to pray about this?" Even if *I* think it's obvious how to pray about it, it's important that they clearly state what *they* want to believe for. And it's important for the rest of the group to be in sync with the direction the prayer should go. If I or one of the others present feel they are asking wrongly, we will make suggestions as how to better pray.

The importance of praying in unity cannot be over-stated as a big contributing factor in seeing answers to our prayers. There is power in unity because God strengthens our faith as He joins our hearts together in one accord.

## When Affinity Groups Are Effective

All of us who were in public ministry were encouraged by Pastor Jack to become part of an affinity group. These are groups in which the members have something important in common, usually their work. For example, we were part of a group who had worldwide ministry in the entertainment industry. There was another group in which everyone had national Christian ministries. These kinds of groups are great because there are certain common experiences, problems, needs, and challenges that benefit from the prayer support of people who understand your situation.

Pastor Jack's main objective for encouraging these groups was for the purpose of strengthening each of our marriages and personal walks with God. He wanted people in public ministry to have solid connections with accountability groups so we could remain strong in the Lord. This was especially effective for those of us who were national or international travelers so we wouldn't be just floating out there, isolated from other strong believers. These groups helped us feel connected, strengthened, and united.

I will never forget one particular meeting of our affinity group. Both men and women were in the same room sharing their prayer requests when one man we had known for quite a while said, "This was the worst week of my entire life." He shared how he and his wife had been having severe financial problems because of setbacks in his work, and they had come to a point of crisis. None of us in the group would ever have suspected anything was wrong if it hadn't been for his sharing in the group that night.

We gathered around the man and his wife and prayed that God would open doors for him to find work, and everyone offered to help them in any way that they could. We prayed that God would reveal His perfect will to him and his wife.

Through that month before the next meeting, it became clear to this couple that God was calling him to give up what he was doing and become a pastor. That is exactly what he did, and he is still a pastor today. If our group had not prayed for him in the powerful way we did that night, I don't believe he would have discerned the leading of the Holy Spirit so quickly. He may even have floundered around for a time, possibly putting his family into bankruptcy before realizing what the Lord's will was for them.

We must not underestimate the power of group prayer in straightening and clearing the path we are to travel and then enabling us to walk on it. It would have been very difficult for that man to give up a career that had been successful if he had not received the strength and clarity God gave him the night we all prayed.

At the church my husband and I now attend in Tennessee, affinity groups are also encouraged. Our pastor, Rice Broocks, encourages people to start them in their workplace or wherever their realm of influence makes it a viable idea. There is a group of doctors who meet for prayer once a week at the hospital where they all work. There are football players who meet together, businessmen who meet, and musicians who gather once a week. I personally know of many moms' groups who meet, married couples who pray, students who gather for regular prayer at their school or dorm. I even know of one group called "Aging Musicians with Menopausal Wives." Anything is possible! (I'm just glad they haven't asked *us* to join.) Any group of three or more people who have something important in common can be turned into this kind of prayer and accountability group.

**The great thing about being in an affinity group** is that it's often easier to find the opportunity to pray together. The people involved have common places where they can meet in the workplace or at a convenient nearby location. The things they have in common make it easier to share concerns and needs without going to great lengths to explain. They understand the issues faced by people in the group. Like home groups, affinity groups allow people to share in ways they otherwise might not.

Another great thing about an affinity group is that it is easier to invite a nonbeliever to attend it. For example, a doctor may be more likely to attend a doctor's prayer group than he would accept an invitation to a church. In that way, these kinds of groups are great evangelistic tools. Countless people who are invited into such an existing group receive the Lord there.

**The *challenge* of being in an affinity group** is that it *can* turn into what may seem like an exclusive club from which others may feel excluded. Or it *can* become a job-networking opportunity instead of a prayer and account-ability group. But this can happen with any kind of group. It's up to the leader to see that it doesn't.

## What You Should Know When Starting a Prayer Group

Would you like to be in a prayer group? If so, you are in for great blessings ahead. Prayer groups enrich your life by connecting you to people in a deep and meaningful way. They are an ongoing source of ministry *to* you and an opportunity for God to work *through* you. They can help you to grow and move into the plans and purposes God has for you.

The way you find a prayer group is to first pray about it. Ask God to help you find the right group for you. Then ask around about groups that get together and pray. If some of the groups you inquire about are already full, don't take that as a rejection. Groups like these fill up very fast.

As you are asking around, you may find other people who are interested in being in a regular prayer group too, and who might be interested in starting one together with you. God may even be asking you to form one yourself. Now, don't get weak-kneed about this. I didn't know what I was doing when I first started either. All I had was the desire to do it and the leading of the Lord. Both of those things came out of my personal prayer time with God. You have access to that instruction in *your* personal prayer time too. So don't be afraid to get before Him and say, "Lord, do You want me to form a prayer group?" Then wait for God's answer. He will impress something upon your heart. Remember, it only takes you and two other people to be a group. Just keep praying and give God time. It will happen.

If you do want to start your own prayer group, here are a few things you should decide first.

**Decide where you can do it.** Can you have the prayer group in your home or apartment, or in the place where you work or go to school? My husband was in a prayer group of four or five men who met at a restaurant and shared their requests over breakfast and prayed right there at the table. Be creative.

**Decide how many people you want to be in it.** More people can increase the power potential, but too many can be unwieldy because there isn't enough time for each person to share and be prayed for adequately. I have found that there should not be more than seven, and five is actually a more manageable number. I've had a prayer group of three that worked well, because all three were very committed and faithful.

*Decide how often you want to meet.* Will it be once a week? Once every other week? Once a month? Will it be a weekday or on the weekend? Will it be morning, afternoon, or evening? How long will you ask each person to commit for? Three months? Six months? Nine months? One year? Pastor Jack and Lloyd Ogilvie, who was at that time the pastor of Hollywood Presbyterian Church before he became chaplain of the U.S. Senate, used to be regular prayer partners. Even with their extremely full calendars as the heads of very large congregations, they still found time to pray together for a couple hours four or five times a year. They would bear their hearts in total transparency and share the burdens and challenges each of them faced. They also organized larger prayer groups that met together several times a year. They saw the importance of praying together and made time for it in their schedules.

*Decide how long the meeting will be.* Two and a half to three hours should be the maximum. Any longer is exhausting. Some people can only afford one hour, and it can be done if the group has only three or four members. Whatever it is, try to keep that time limit as strictly as possible. It helps people to plan, and they will more likely be consistent in coming if you are consistent in watching the time.

*Decide who will be in the group.* Remember, this is *God's* prayer group, so only He knows who will make the best prayer partners. Ask Him to show you. And give people the freedom to say no when you ask them to join. This is a big commitment, and not everyone can do it. I usually give people a week or two to pray about it before they give me an answer. If someone says no, that does not mean there is anything wrong with you or your idea; it just means that person is not the right one for your group or they are not ready yet.

If you are going to start a prayer group of your own, here are seven helpful guidelines to keep things flowing smoothly. I learned these things the hard way so you won't have to now.

### 1. Have a plan.

You don't have to stay *strictly* with your plan if you need to alter it, but you do need to have one to begin with. It makes the other people in the group feel more secure because they know what to expect. For example, at the beginning of each prayer group, I read from the Bible for about three minutes in order to get people's hearts in tune and on the same page, so to speak. Then we all get on our knees and sing worship and praise songs and speak praise to God for about 20 minutes.

When we finish the worship time, we sit back down and begin with the person whose turn it is to go first. The way I have determined that is by putting the last names in alphabetical order and starting with a different person each week, proceeding alphabetically. That means the one who went last this week will go first the next week. This keeps the same person from always ending up last, and it saves the group a good ten minutes trying to decide who should go first.

### 2. Choose praise and worship songs that everyone knows.

You will not have a lot of time for worship, and everyone needs to be able to get into it right away. Also, people are often more self-conscious singing in a small group, and they don't want their voices to stand out in case they make a mistake. I usually lead out with one song in the beginning, and tell the people in the group to lead out in any praise song that comes to their hearts as they feel led. It is completely spontaneous, and that way no one has to prepare a worship service. Some women always lead out, some never do. Whether they do or not doesn't matter. Everyone should be comfortable either way. If no one in your group feels they can sing or lead out in a song, then get a tape or CD that has worship songs on it that you like and sing along to it.

Once you get into it, it's easy to spend a long time in worship, so as the leader you always have to keep an eye on the time. A time of worship is very important because God inhabits your praises, and you are inviting His presence to soften your hearts so you can receive from Him. It prepares your hearts for the coming prayer time.

### 3. Encourage people in the group to have their requests prepared before the prayer time.

Because time is usually limited and it is way too easy to go overtime on everything in a group like this, encourage your members to have their requests listed on a piece of paper *before* they come. That way it clarifies the requests in their mind enough to be able to verbalize them clearly for the others. It can take several minutes for someone just to figure out what their prayer requests are if they haven't given them any thought beforehand.

### 4. Don't allow people to take more time sharing their request than they do praying about them.

If someone spends 25 minutes giving their request and allows 5 minutes for prayer, they are getting shortchanged. The prayer time should be at least equal to if not longer than the sharing time. When I had five women in my group, they each had 30 minutes. This meant they had about 10 minutes to share their needs and about 20 minutes to be prayed for. There is tremendous power when five people pray for one person, so you want to give everyone time to take advantage of this unique opportunity.

### 5. Stress the importance of confidentiality.

Impress on the members of the group how important it is to not be discussing another's prayer requests, or any details of what they share in the group, with anyone *outside* the group. One would think people would know to do that out of common decency or out of respect and love for that person. But unfortunately not everyone does. You would be surprised at the seemingly innocent ways people can justify hurtful gossip. Betraying a confidence will destroy a prayer group faster than anything else.

That is the reason you have to carefully weigh the trust factor when asking people to be in a prayer group. It's not about secrecy, it's about maturity. It's about not doing to others what you would not want done to you. You don't want to pray with someone who will gossip about the intimate details of your life. In all my years of prayer partners, there have been only a couple incidents where someone listened to the intimate details of a prayer request and then repeated it to others outside the prayer group. In each case, I stopped the group immediately. It grieved me that someone who listened to another's pain would hurt that person further by betraying a confidence.

### 6. Don't allow any one person to dominate the rest of the group.

There will always be people who talk more than others, so be careful not to let the ones who are most talkative or needy take up more than their allotted time. If they do, it will prevent others from being able to give their requests and be prayed for adequately. And usually the ones who are quiet will not stick up for themselves and demand equal time. They will suffer in silence and eventually drop out. It is up to you, the leader, to watch out for this and make sure it doesn't happen. That's why it's good to keep a clock handy and move things along when someone has reached their time limit. Warn them in advance that you are going to do this. This is a very important issue, because if the time factor gets out of control, people may leave your prayer group because of it.

### 7. *Do not talk about other people.*

The only time a person should talk or pray about other people who are not in the group is if those people pertain directly to their own life. That is, if another person is affecting your life adversely and you need prayer for that specific situation. It is of utmost importance that these groups not turn into gossip fests. This is not a setting in which anyone should bring up someone else's marriage problem unless that person has specifically requested that the group pray for this need. Just be wise. There is great potential for pain on all sides if this issue is not handled properly.

ᔐ ᔐ ᔐ

Many of my prayer partners have told me that one of the best things about being in our prayer group was having the opportunity to pray regularly about something for as long as it took. In other words, they saw the value of continuing to press through in prayer until they saw answers. When praying alone, we can sometimes become discouraged and give up too soon. Also, praying together forces us to verbalize our prayer needs and teaches us how to allow other people to share our burdens. We gain strength, encouragement, and faith each time we hear others pray for us, and corporate prayer opens up a wonderful flow of God's blessings into our life.

In all of my prayer groups, there were people who shared from the deepest recesses of their souls. They exposed the gut-wrenching nakedness of hurts and needs so deep they would only allow the most trusted hearts to share it. These are people who stood with me when I needed to do the same. As a group we encouraged one another to not give up when it seemed the answer would never come. These are people I know I could call for prayer or help and in an instant they would be there—no matter how long it had been since I had last seen them. And they know I will be there for them in that way too. There is a bond of love between us that is eternal.

The truth is, you always grow to love the people you pray for. That's because you develop God's heart of love for them. Don't pass up the chance to experience that.

## Prayer Power

Lord, I ask that You would help me find a group of strong believers with whom I can pray regularly. Lead me to people who have their foundation built solidly on the Word of God and who have strong faith to believe for answers to their prayers. Show me if I am to lead such a group. If so, prepare me to do it well. Tell me when it should be and whom I should invite into it. Lead me to people who can make that kind of commitment and be consistent. May this prayer group be a positive and life-changing experience for everyone who is part of it.

Anytime I pray with others in a group, help us to come to a place of complete unity with one another. May we always be in one accord so that our prayers are powerful.

Help us to submit to one another in the fear of God (Ephesians 5:21). Help us to "walk by the same rule" and "be of the same mind" (Philippians 3:16). Enable us to "stand fast in one spirit, with one mind striving together for the faith of the gospel" (Philippians 1:27). Help us to "be kindly affectionate to one another with brotherly love, in honor giving preference to one another; not lagging in diligence, fervent in spirit, serving the Lord; rejoicing in hope, patient in tribulation, continuing steadfastly in prayer" (Romans 12:10-12).

Teach me how to pray effectively for other people. I want to always pray with Your clear leading and guidance. When I pray, give me great faith to believe for the answers. I know that without faith it is impossible to please You (Hebrews 11:6), and I want to please You more than anything else. Help me to be the kind of person who, by joining with others, is able to resist the onslaught of the enemy when he comes upon our lives like a torrential flash flood. May my faith be so strong that it gives rise to faith in others and encourages them to stand strong. In Jesus' name I pray.

〜 〜 〜

## Word Power

Be of the same mind toward one another. Do not set your mind on high things, but associate with the humble. Do not be wise in your own opinion.

ROMANS 12:16

Confess your trespasses to one another, and
pray for one another, that you may be healed.
The effective, fervent prayer of a righteous
man avails much.

JAMES 5:16

Therefore if there is any consolation in Christ, if
any comfort of love, if any fellowship of the
Spirit, if any affection and mercy, fulfill my joy
by being like-minded, having the same love,
being of one accord, of one mind. Let nothing
be done through selfish ambition or conceit,
but in lowliness of mind let each esteem others
better than himself. Let each of you look out
not only for his own interests, but also
for the interests of others.

PHILIPPIANS 2:1-4

I, therefore, the prisoner of the Lord, beseech
you to walk worthy of the calling with which
you were called, with all lowliness and gentleness, with longsuffering, bearing with one
another in love, endeavoring to keep the unity
of the Spirit in the bond of peace.

EPHESIANS 4:1-3

Without faith it is impossible to please Him, for
he who comes to God must believe that He is,
and that He is a rewarder of those who
diligently seek Him.

HEBREWS 11:6

# Five

# The Power
# of a Praying
# Church

For the duration of my first pregnancy, I suffered with debilitating pain and nausea. Although my doctor told me I would not likely have that same problem again, my second pregnancy was even worse. The pain and nausea were so bad, in fact, that I could not eat much of anything for months, and so I had to be hospitalized and put on intravenous feeding. When my veins finally gave out, the doctor sent me home, saying there was nothing more he could do. I was discharged from the hospital on Sunday in the seventh month of my pregnancy, sicker and weaker than ever.

Throughout the seemingly endless months of my struggle, many individuals prayed for me and some even came to the hospital to do it. On the Saturday before I was released, Pastor Jack visited me at the hospital and prayed for me too. I knew that the prayers of these faithful people had sustained me and the baby through that time, but still I felt discouraged about the future because I wasn't getting any better.

When I arrived home that Sunday, my husband helped me back into the bed where I had been for months. Our close friends Bob and Sally arrived soon after that in order to prepare dinner for our two families. Everyone knew I would not be eating with them.

At about 6:30 that evening, I was lying in my bed listening to people talking in the kitchen as they finished dinner. For months I had felt too sick to read or even watch television, so all I could do was lie still in agony and think longingly about the simple things I used to take for granted, like sitting at a table and eating with friends.

Suddenly I felt the strangest sensation. It was the complete absence of all the nausea and pain. I laid there for a few moments, barely breathing, waiting for it to come back. When it didn't, I sat up in bed and waited some more. I could hardly believe it had not returned. I pulled back the covers and slowly sat up on the edge of the bed with my feet on the floor and waited for a few more minutes. When nothing changed, I stood and walked carefully to the bathroom connected to my bedroom and looked in the mirror. It shocked me to see how extremely thin, frail, gaunt, and pale I had become. Still, I did not feel any nausea or pain.

I walked cautiously to the bed and sat down again, as if any sudden movement might bring it all back. I must have stayed there five minutes before I finally became brave enough to venture outside the bedroom, down the hall, and past the den where my husband was lying on the couch watching television.

"What are you doing up?" he asked, sitting upright in disbelief.

"I don't know what's happened, but I feel different," I answered and kept walking to where Sally was putting the finishing touches on the kitchen cleanup.

"What are you doing up?" she asked in astonishment. By that time Michael and Bob had followed me in from the den.

"I don't know what happened, but all of a sudden I feel totally fine," I said.

Michael pulled out a chair for me to sit at the table as Sally asked, "Do you want something to eat?"

"Yes," I said. "Quick, before it comes back again."

Within a half minute she gave me a small bowl of sliced pears and a dry piece of warm toast, which I ate slowly and carefully. It was the best meal I could remember eating in months. Actually, it was the *only* meal I could remember eating in months. I kept it down, and we all rejoiced over this miraculous reprieve. Twenty minutes later I went back to bed to get some desperately needed sleep before the pain and nausea returned.

When I awoke Monday morning I still felt fine. I talked with Michael about whether I should call Pastor Jack to tell him what happened, but then I thought better of it. I decided to wait one more day just to be sure.

On Tuesday morning when I again woke up feeling good, I knew it was time to let Pastor Jack know. I called him and recounted the entire story of what happened.

"What time was that on Sunday night?" he asked.

"It was about 6:30," I said.

"That was the same time the entire congregation was praying for you in the Sunday evening service," he explained in a voice filled with delight.

"Really? The whole congregation prayed for me?" I asked in astonishment. It had become quite a large assembly of people by that time.

"Yes, didn't anyone tell you?" he asked in surprise. "I was sure someone would have called to let you know."

"No, no one called," I answered, choking back tears of gratefulness. "Thank you so much for doing that—for having all those people pray for me."

"Praise God, this is a miracle!" he exclaimed.

"Do you really think so?" I asked, still hesitant to believe that I was actually healed.

"Yes!" he said emphatically. "I know so!"

He was right. From that time on, I was free of the suffering. And how else could this miraculous turn of events be explained, except that it was a result of prayer? Suggesting it was merely a *coincidence* that after seven months of agony I was suddenly healed at the same time the congregation prayed for me is ridiculous. Even my doctor thought it was astounding when I told him what happened. He said he had never seen a condition so bad disappear so quickly. I knew it was a miracle that happened as a result of the prayers of faithful believers.

Because of that experience, I came to see that the power of a praying church is a formidable force with unlimited possibilities. It is a resource that has yet to be tapped to its fullest. And tap it we must. For the time is upon us when we as a believing people must draw on that resource and learn to pray in Holy Spirit-led-and-enabled power. The *salvation* of our world—in every meaning of the word—depends on it. May God help us understand the consequences if we don't.

༄ ༄ ༄

After Jesus was crucified and resurrected, a group of 120 people prayed together every day and became the first recorded church of the New Testament. They were unified in their beliefs, and they moved "with one accord in prayer" (Acts 1:14). The very first church was a *praying church*.

A little later, after the outpouring of the Holy Spirit, 3000 people were saved, and they, too, "continued steadfastly...in prayers" (Acts 2:42). When some of these people asked God to give them the boldness they needed in order to speak His Word and see signs and wonders done in Jesus' name, God answered them in power. "When they had prayed, the place where they were assembled together was shaken; and they were all filled with the Holy Spirit, and they spoke the word of God with boldness" (Acts 4:31). This early church had one long continuous prayer meeting, and when they prayed, things happened.

*The power of the church today is still prayer.* And we, the body of Christ, can also be shaken by the manifest power of God. We can see things shaken up in the world around us if we are willing to pray as fervently and as unceasingly as the early church did, mirroring also their faith and unity.

"There are certain dynamics to that kind of prayer meeting which are pivotal to making it work," explained Pastor Jack. "One of the things that has to happen is people must come to a conviction about the invisible life. They need to be unified in believing that the invisible realm is real, and that they have been given a place of privileged authority and access in it. Most people know they should pray, but many don't believe it's going to make any difference. If they recognize there is a very real penetration in the invisible realm, it emboldens them and they can believe with greater faith. Jesus came to change things, to save people, to heal the sick, to transform families and circumstances, and to impact nations with a moral turnaround in the souls of people. And the power of a praying church is the key to that."

## Building a House for God's Presence

I don't believe I ever went through a worship service at the church when I did not weep. It was because I sensed the presence of God so strongly.

One of my favorite things about the Lord is that He promises whenever we worship Him, we are establishing a place for His presence to come and dwell. What could be more wonderful than to have God's Spirit reside in our midst? And this can happen in our home, in our church, on a mountaintop, in a field, out at sea, or all places in between. That's because when we worship God, He is enthroned in our praises (Psalm 22:3). What other religion can boast of a God like that?

Pastor Jack taught us that there are three dimensions of the presence of God revealed in the Bible: the *omnipresence*, the *promise presence*, and the *manifest presence*.

"There are always purists who will say that 'God's everywhere, so don't talk to me about the presence of God,' and that's true," he said. "There is the *omnipresence of God*, which affects everyone because He is everywhere. But the Bible makes it clear that there are two other dimensions of God's presence. The *promise presence of God*, which comes when He guides us, walks with us, and speaks to our hearts, and the *manifest presence of God*, which is seen at a group level when people move together in a spirit of worship that welcomes the presence of God's power."

The way to build a house for God's manifest presence is through worship. When people welcome Him with praise and worship, His manifest presence comes in power. He will not come in the *fullness* of His presence if we don't give Him a place to dwell in our worship.

Every congregation makes a choice as to what degree they want the presence of God in their midst by the importance they assign to worshiping Him.

As the church of the Lord in this world, we are in a battle against forces of evil that want to see us brought down. But the Bible promises we are more than conquerors and our victory is certain (Romans 8:37). When we praise God, the Holy Spirit comes in power and Satan is defeated. Everything that tries to destroy each one of us, like sickness, pain, poverty, sin, discouragement, strife, and failure, can be reversed with praise. When we worship God, He works powerfully to defeat anything that opposes us.

"There is peace and a resource of strength and confidence in the presence of God, no matter what else happens in the world around us," said Pastor Jack. "But it doesn't happen without praise and worship. Praise destroys the atmosphere in which sickness, defeat, futility, and discouragement flourish. Praise upsets the climate which furthers the growth of so much of life's suffering, confusion, turmoil, and strife. Praise beats out hell's fire and breathes heaven's life into the vacuum death produces on earth. God's power is like a tornado that sweeps away the obstacles of sin, self, sickness, and Satan."

We are not just trying to get God's attention and stir up God's interest by praising Him. He is already attentive and interested. We are not just trying to flatter Him so He will favor us and answer our prayers. He already favors us and has promised to answer our prayers. By praising Him, we are expressing our love and reverence toward Him, and being obedient to what He asks us to do.

"The Word of God does not command us to thank God for every pain, evil, tragedy, or trouble," explained Pastor Jack. "Instead it tells us to never let circumstances dampen our praise. It does not say *for* everything give thanks, but *in* everything give thanks. Whatever the situation, irrespective of how bleak, we are to praise God that He is greater than our circumstances and that His love guarantees our triumph over or through them."

Often in church at the end of the worship time, Pastor Jack would ask us all to join hands with the people on either side of us and bridge the aisles. Then he would lead us in prayer about a specific issue. Every time we did that, I could feel the strong unity in the people and the power of God's Spirit flowing through us. Then with our hands still joined, he would ask us to raise our hands and sing praise to the Lord. The power of that moment of corporate worship was palpable and immeasurable, and there was no question that the presence of God had found a home.

Building a house for God's presence happens when we set ourselves to worship God *His* way and make it our *first* priority. That means each of us as individuals must make that a priority in our lives as well. Not only do we need to be a part of corporate worship times in our church services or other meetings where believers are gathered to worship God, but it's important that we praise and worship Him countless times throughout our day. Worship is a form of prayer. Seeing power in our prayers begins there.

## Building a People to Do His Work

"I'm not interested in building a big *church,* I'm interested in building big *people,*" Pastor Jack told us time and again throughout the years I was one of his sheep. He never thought about how to grow a congregation of many because he was too busy trying to grow us up as individuals to be all God created us to be. We were constantly being stretched spiritually and personally, and for us it became a way of life. In spite of that, church attendance always grew way beyond what we had room for. Even the addition of multiple services and the acquisition of more properties never seemed to keep up with it.

During this time, I learned that the church is not just a building. The church is the people. You and I and millions of others who believe in Jesus make up the church. The church *building* is a place where believers can gather to be nurtured, grown, and prepared to go out and do God's work.

*Everyone in the church—the body of Christ, the believers*—has a purpose for their lives. And God has placed gifts, talents, and abilities in each one of us in order to accomplish that purpose (Ephesians 4:8-16). *Belonging to a church—a local body of believers, a congregation*—led by godly leaders who will help you grow, is the most effective way to identify and develop those gifts and become an effective person for God's kingdom. Through this church family, God will teach you about Himself and His plans for your life.

"The church is not built by skilled leadership. The church is built by Jesus," explained Pastor Jack. "But leaders are there to cultivate understanding in the people. What characterizes much of the church in the world is that people think of pastors or clergy as hired professionals who will be godly in their behalf. They look to their leaders to *do* church, and they *go* to church so church can happen *to* them. In doing that, people don't think of themselves as instruments for penetrating the world with the life of Jesus. But the church is not an organization, it is an organism. And God's plan is that the leaders nurture in people a dimension of who they were created to be."

It's important that you not lose sight of the fact that you are part of the greater body of Christ. If you don't understand this, you will tend to think of yourself as a layman, someone who is "just" a mom or dad, or "just" a housewife, schoolteacher, fireman, or student, or "just" an office worker, soldier, plumber, or salesperson. You won't see yourself as a tool of God's love and power right where you are, no matter where that is or what you're doing for a living. Being in church and praying with other believers helps you to see that you are connected to, and a part of, what God is doing on the earth.

That's why every time you come to church, something discernable—something of growth—should be taking place inside of you through the teaching, worship, and prayer. Whenever you are with the body of Christ, you should feel refreshed, renewed, encouraged, and edified.

If you don't believe any of those things are happening to you, or that you are not being equipped to become all you were created to be, then ask God if you are in the right church. He has a specific church family for you, so ask Him where that is. He will show you.

"The place of the believer in perceiving himself as a person who has great potential in prayer is fundamental to what the church is to be,", said Pastor Jack. "At a prayer meeting in the early church at Antioch, the Lord set forth a plan that changed the world (Acts 13:1-3). Members of that congregation recognized that change would involve two things: their response to the Holy Spirit that brought them to prayer and fasting, and their sending forth ministry. And the world *was* changed. It is an observable fact that history turned on the basis of that prayer meeting in Antioch, Syria, nearly 2000 years ago. Any historical analysis shows that the flow of events that has shaped the world as we know it today—notably Western civilization—can be directly traced to that prayer meeting.

"People who pray and understand who they have been made to be in Christ set the direction of history of their world—be it local, regional, national, or international. Most of the believing church today thinks of faith in Jesus Christ as an escape. But God says He wants us to be instruments of redemption and intercessory prayer, and ministry will flow out of that."

I have learned one thing for certain in the 30-plus years I have walked with the Lord: *It's impossible to grow and develop to your fullest potential independently of other believers.* It can't be "just me and God all the way." We have a mutual dependence upon one another because we are defined and refined within the context of a local body of believers.

"There are many people who would like to have a privatized walk with God," said Pastor Jack. "The intimacy of our private walk with the Lord is a very wonderful part of our life, but if that's all you have, you do not have a developing Christian life. Too easily, it can wither. We will focus on ourselves. Sadly, there are people who live that way and consider it spiritual: withdrawing into their own world. This is somewhat the same as the escapist lifestyle that characterized the spiritual pursuit of many leaders that eventuated in the Dark Ages. The culture became spiritually dark because people forgot how the Light spreads. That lifestyle was called monasticism—people seeking private illumination from God but failing to be united with other believers to become mutually warmed and ignited. When we join with other believers, we can become an 'on fire' church that not only prays with power, but reaches out with God's love."

*Building a people to do God's work happens in the local church when we are connected to and grow with the rest of the congregation. It is within that context that we find who we are created to be and what we are created to do.*

One of the most important things about being in a spiritual family is finding power in prayer through unity. When a husband and wife are in unity, their marriage is strong. And when children are in unity with their parents and with each other, the family stays strong. It's the same with spiritual family. When the leaders are in unity, and the believers are in unity with them and with each other, there is a dynamic that adds power to their prayers and the confidence that God will answer in power.

## Building a Force That Is Irresistible

When I started going to the midweek service on Wednesday nights at church, I found the same life-changing worship and great teaching that were present on Sunday mornings. But I also learned how to truly intercede for people and situations. In our prayer circles we were each handed cards upon which were written specific prayer requests from people in the congregation, in the city, in the nation, and all over the world. These people had called or written to ask the church to pray. We also prayed for issues and situations in the world which the pastor or others brought to our attention. Prayer time lasted a lot longer on Wednesday nights—perhaps 30 minutes—because there were always so many things to pray about. And we saw amazing answers to prayer—especially for our city.

In the late 1980s there was a severe drought in Southern California. This particular drought was especially bad because there had been hardly any rain for a number of years. It became so bad, in fact, that we were put on water rationing. If you have never experienced this kind of thing before, it is frightening. You can't water your plants, lawn, or garden, so everything dies. You can't flush your toilet or take a shower when you want to, so it is highly inconvenient. If you are not diligent to keep bottled water on hand, you might not have enough to drink. And if you use more than the allotted amount of water, you will not only pay an exorbitant price, but your water will be completely shut off. And there is nothing you can do about it. During a drought, there is no way to get more water in the amounts you need.

In one of our Wednesday night prayer meetings, the Lord moved on Anna Hayford's heart to share a picture the Lord had given her as she was watching a local newscast. The weatherman reported that a high-pressure cell had been sitting over the four corners of the area and had not moved for a very long time. As Anna watched the report, the Lord put in her heart that the congregation should pray against the spirit that was resisting the blessing of rain and keeping that cell from moving. And we were to do this even though we were now into the month of March, which meant that the rainy season for Southern California had passed.

Pastor Jack reminded us of the dynamic relationship between the natural and the spiritual realm, and how God spoke to the people of ancient Judah. He told them that whenever people fail to sustain worship to the Lord, "on them there will be no rain" (Zechariah 14:17). We concluded from this principle that if we *did* worship God as intercessors, there was reason to believe we could expect that there *would* be rain. We trusted that by praising and exalting the Lord, and by praying specifically about this, we could break whatever was keeping that pressure cell from moving out and we could have rain, even though it was not the season for it.

Remarkably, that very weatherman who gave the forecast just happened to be visiting our church that night, and he heard all Anna said. He observed the people worshiping God, and he heard Pastor Jack praying that anything obstructing the movement of the weather cell would move out and that rain would come. He was amazed to hear this kind of thing actually being prayed about at church.

Though the cell had been entrenched for *weeks,* blocking potential weather patterns that would bring rain, in less than 48 hours that cell *did* move and rain began to pour upon the city in abundance. In fact, it turned out to be the rainiest month of March in the history of Los Angeles. Enough rain fell to cover the entire season. When the weatherman saw what happened to the weather after that night of prayer at church, he mentioned it on television one evening during his weather report.

"You know this rain we are having?" he asked. "I was at a church that prayed for this very thing to happen—the movement of this cell and the coming of this rain."

Because it was such a powerful testimony to him, he later came back to church and received the Lord. He recognized there was no way such rain would naturally have come because it normally rains very little in March in Southern California. Because of those rains, the news and weather reporters in Los Angeles dubbed that year's phenomena as "Miracle March." It was called that even by those who knew nothing about what happened at the church.

That whole experience changed all of us who prayed. First of all, it made us very aware of how terrible it must be for people in countries experiencing ongoing severe drought. We had new compassion and motivation to pray for people in that kind of situation. Second, we never complained about rainy days again. And third, we learned that prayer was something even powerful forces of nature couldn't resist.

Don't get me wrong. When I relate these answers to prayers the church prayed, I'm not saying they were only because of *our* church praying. I'm sure God called other people and other churches to pray too. I'm saying that those of us who were there for that night of prayer knew how much of a miracle those rains were. We saw how God answers prayer when people are unified in the spirit of praise and they pray in power.

Some people may question that God would really change the weather because people prayed. But He did it in the Bible. "Elijah was a man with a nature like ours, and he prayed earnestly that it would not rain; and it did not rain on the land for three years and six months. And he prayed again, and the heaven gave rain, and the earth produced its fruit" (James 5:17-18). The Bible also says that "with God nothing will be impossible" (Luke 1:37) and "Jesus Christ is the same yesterday, today, and forever" (Hebrews 13:8). What more do we need to know?

〜 〜 〜

During the 40 years I lived in Los Angeles, I survived many earthquakes. We expected them. The Bible says the earth is going to have them. Seismologists tell us that there is a big one coming in California. And numerous authors have prophesied in books about future earthquakes. But Pastor Jack taught us that while we needed to find our place of refuge in the Lord no matter what happened, we should see these predictions as motivation to pray.

"The Bible nowhere exempts seismic activity as a subject for the intercessory prayers of God's people," said Pastor Jack. "If we can pray, and by God's grace there can come a ceasing of storms; if we can pray and by God's power divert hurricanes, if we can pray and invoke rain where there's been drought, then there is no reason to feel it is presumptuous to pray about earthquakes. Psalm 115:16 says the heavens are given to the Lord, but the earth He has given to the children of men. The redeemed sons and daughters of God have a right to expect that it is their privilege to pray about what could be disastrous and see it ameliorated in either of two ways. Either through praying that there come a reduction of the impact of it, or if it comes with all its impact, that there be redemption and healing in the situation."

You may wonder, "If that's true and people were praying, then why did the 1994 earthquake happen in Northridge? Did people stop praying that day?"

As long as I lived in Northridge, I prayed daily for protection from earthquakes. And I know countless other people were praying that way as well. I believe that's why there were relatively few deaths in spite of how massive and violent that earthquake was. There could have been thousands, but there were only a few. If no one was praying, the situation might have been much worse.

If something bad happens in your city, that doesn't necessarily mean people were not praying. God is not sitting up in heaven thinking up traumatic circumstances and events that will teach us a lesson. He is waiting for us to come to a place of repentance over our prayerlessness and lack of faith in His ability to answer our prayers. He is waiting for us to wake up and become a force so strong that neither the forces of hell nor the forces of nature can resist it.

Some of the other things our church prayed about were that the police force would be strong and good and able to bring down the crime rate, that outbreaks of contagious disease would be stopped, that forest fires would be brought under control, that righteous city leaders would be elected, that honest and godly judges would be appointed, that there would be peace in our neighborhoods, and that other churches all over the city would flourish.

Of course we always prayed for situations outside of our city that we knew needed a miraculous touch from God.

When Dayna Curry and Heather Mercer were imprisoned in Afghanistan, Pastor Jack's church in Los Angeles prayed for them, the church I attend now in Tennessee prayed for them, their own churches prayed for them, and countless churches all over the nation and the world prayed for them. After we received news that they were finally set free and brought home safely, millions of us everywhere wept and thanked God for that incredible answer to prayer.

Months after their release, I was on a book tour and so were they. I ran into Heather and Dayna a number of times at the different TV and radio studios where we were being interviewed. Every time I talked with them and gave them a hug, I choked up with tears because I knew I was embracing a miracle. The safe release of Heather and Dayna is one of the best and most beautiful testimonies of the irresistible power of a praying church. No plan of hell can prevail against it.

## Breaking Down Denominational Walls

How do you compare apples, oranges, pears, blueberries, cherries, papayas, and bananas? Each one has its own great, distinct flavor. But they are all fruit. And when combined, they make a great fruit salad. That's the way it should be with denominations. The purpose of denominations should be to organize believers into distinct families, not to erect walls that separate the body of Christ.

There is nothing wrong with having distinct denominations in the church any more than there was anything wrong with having different tribes in Israel in the Old Testament. But when we become so enamored of our own tribe, or denomination, that we fail to acknowledge we have brothers and sisters in other tribes and we are all Israel, then it becomes a problem. God doesn't want us to disrespect other tribes, building walls of attitude toward them and thinking it's righteous. He wants us to love one another because we are all part of Christ's body.

People build denominational walls because they're afraid someone will go over to another tribe. And in some cases, people are given the idea that if they go to another tribe, they may not even be in Israel at all. We must pray that this mindset of denominational separatism, which puts up walls between people when the body of Christ should be coming together, will be replaced by an appreciation of our differences. Different flavors—one salad.

Jesus said that the way the world will know that we are His disciples is by our love for one another (John 13:34-35). In too many parts of the church, people aren't seeing it. They see us closing ranks and loving our own.

They see us not reaching out to others who are different in some way from us. They see us fighting among ourselves.

One of the questions I am most often asked by unbelievers is, "What is the purpose of denominations? I don't get it. Why do you need them? Why is one denomination so critical of another?"

Every time I try to explain it, I find myself wondering the same thing. Why do we focus so adamantly on our differences instead of celebrating the wonderful and powerful things we have in common?

While we don't believe in an "anything goes" grounds for unity, many godly leaders have agreed that, irrespective of denominational affiliation, they could band together under a statement that focuses on biblical basics that any Christian can agree to. Such things as: the deity of our Lord Jesus, His virgin birth, His sinless life, His atoning death on the cross, His resurrection; or that God is one God, externally existent in the three persons of the Father, the Son, and the Holy Spirit; or that the Bible is the inspired and infallible Word of God; or when we believe in and receive Jesus, then we will have an eternal future with Him in heaven. On grounds like these, is there not room for us to get together in the love of God and in the name of Jesus in order to move in the power of unified prayer?

I see the younger generation ready for that way of thinking. Fortunately, many of them are determined to bring change and unity in that regard.

"There are many denominations all over the nation and the world, with many worthy ministries and missions being realized in each one," said Pastor Jack. "And if I have ever felt things on the brink of breakthrough with regard to division, it is now. A bridging of the breach and recovery of relationship calls for one person at a time to reach out in the gentleness of Jesus to people of other church traditions and see church fellowship broadly established in the body of Christ."

In order to do that we need to focus on what we *agree* on instead of fighting over issues where we don't see eye to eye. We have to be more concerned with bringing unbelievers to the Lord than we are with proving to other believers we are more right—or more righteous—than they are.

"There is never any agreement in the realm of darkness," explained Pastor Jack. "Though there are times when the hosts of hell marshal together, it is not because they 'agree,' but because they are chained together. That's why the enemy resists any attempts at unifying the body of Christ. But in Christ, the Bible says two or three in agreement have a dynamic in the Holy Spirit of unity that can break through the adversary's opposition."

The enemy's goal is to create division whenever and wherever he can because he doesn't want us coming together. When two of even the weakest saints are in agreement, he cannot withstand it. And when the whole church prays together, his defeat is devastating.

The beauty of a rainbow is when all the colors are seen together. People are beginning to recognize that. Jesus is bringing His church together magnificently, and this is happening with the breaking down of denominational walls. Such organizations as The National Day of Prayer, Promise Keepers (for men), the Billy Graham Evangelistic Crusades, See You at the Pole (for kids in junior high and high school), the Luis Palau Festivals, Greg Laurie Harvest Crusades, and many wonderful national women's conferences are just a few good examples of large praying groups who have broken down denominational walls and crossed all barriers to accomplish great things for God's kingdom. We need more of that in our world. It would be good for each of us to become involved in organizations like these.

When pastors come to know one another as people and not as denominational symbols, things begin to change. They start to recognize that they have common goals and they all face similar challenges. They no longer think in terms of competition or being more right than someone else. They think instead of being on the same team. Pastor Jack told the congregation about his own struggle with this very thing when he first came to the church.

"I didn't think I was sectarian," said Pastor Jack. "But when Anna and I came to this church, it was tiny. And down the street was one of the ten largest churches in America at that time. I remember the first Sunday at our new little church. I was standing out on the front steps of the sanctuary, waiting for people to arrive so I could greet them. About thirty people showed up. But I saw countless cars streaming past our church and going to that big church down the street."

A couple of weeks later, Pastor Jack was driving down the street from our church, and he stopped at a red light in front of that big church. As he sat in the car waiting for the light to turn green, he noticed that the side of his face toward the church building burned like fire. Instantly, he recognized the Lord was exposing an attitude he had about that big church—one he didn't even realize had evolved in his heart. He described the encounter as a conversation between himself and the Lord, one which resulted in his being strongly corrected yet greatly released.

Feeling the unexplainable burning, he inquired, "Lord, I know what I feel is not right, so what should I do?"

The Lord spoke to his heart saying, "You could at least begin by looking at the building."

So he turned and looked at the church and said, "What should I do now, Lord?"

"I'm calling you to pray for what I'm doing at that church." The words were powerfully impressed upon his heart. "So great is the work I'm doing there, the pastors in that church can't keep up with it. However, though these are not part of your flock, you are one of My shepherds, and I'm calling you to pray."

"A miracle happened in my heart in that instant," explained Pastor Jack to our congregation, "and I *loved* that church. If I had been wheelchair-bound and got up and started walking, it would have been no less a miracle to me. That's because attitudes in the heart can sometimes be just as hard to change as a physical affliction. And what astounded me during the weeks that followed was that when I drove by other churches, I realized I now felt the same way about them.

"God had really done something in my heart. It wasn't that I had previously felt hatred, anger, or even competition. But I had categories I put people in. For example, driving by a church with a religious tradition I could not accept, I presumed I was justified in supposing God disapproved of them too. But in one specific instance, the Lord whetted my heart with a love I never thought I would feel. He spoke to me, saying, 'How could you think that I would not want to bless a church where *every morning* the testimony of the blood of my Son is lifted at the altar of worship?'"

Just as states should not have barriers in a country, denominations should not have barriers in the body of Christ. Denominations should organize people into families, but we must seek to avoid a spirit that divides people into competing camps. When unbelievers see Christians fighting among themselves, they dismiss us as irrelevant. I know because when I was a nonbeliever, I used to have a critical attitude about that too. We can't bring a message of hope and peace to others when we act as though we don't have one ourselves.

The breaking down of denominational barriers starts with people like you and me praying together for unity in the body of Christ. And we must also reach out to touch others in different denominations. We can pray that church leaders and pastors will bring people of every denomination in a city together to pray. When that occurs, walls will come down, unity will rise, and powerful things will happen.

## Breaking Down Racial and Cultural Barriers

One of the greatest things I noticed about Pastor Jack's ministry was that the people who attended his congregation were of every culture, race, and color. It's the same in the church I attend now in Tennessee, and I'm seeing it more and more at churches wherever I travel. Everyone who comes to church senses the love of God being extended to them. And I know it is because the pastors and leaders in these churches have deliberately reached out to *all* people.

One of the most powerful events I have witnessed, one that broke down cultural, racial, and denominational barriers, happened when Pastor Jack and Pastor Lloyd Ogilvie invited a group of churches together to unite in prayer and seek the welfare of our city. Lloyd Ogilvie was then the pastor of Hollywood Presbyterian Church, and this was not long before he became the chaplain of the United States Senate.

It all started when Pastor Jack invited a number of leaders and pastors in Los Angeles to come together for a prayer breakfast on our church property. After the meal, he told them the reason he had invited them. He explained his vision that they would pray together for the city. He outlined issues of deep need for Los Angeles and then how they could begin to move together in a continuous pursuit of networking with hundreds of pastors in prayer. When he finished, in that instant there was an incredibly dramatic earthquake! It wasn't a damaging one, but it was a strong, significant jolt that rocked the room, rattling dishes and silverware on their breakfast tables. It certainly got everyone's attention, and all who were present recognized it as more than coincidence. As a result, feeling God was calling them together, they agreed to do it. (I'm sure I would have too!)

Shortly after that, Pastor Jack teamed up with Lloyd Ogilvie, and they invited more pastors to come to a similar prayer meeting at Pastor Ogilvie's church in Hollywood. It was so successful that they decided to hold this same kind of meeting three times a year, and each time they met, the attendance increased.

In the most memorable meeting I have ever attended, Pastor Hayford and Pastor Ogilvie invited every pastor in the city, along with leaders of their congregations to come together for a giant prayer meeting called "Love L.A." The purpose of this gathering was to unite all churches to pray for the city. It was held in an enormous church located in the urban part of Los Angeles. Ten thousand people came, representing hundreds of congregations and every racial and denominational type.

The moment I walked into the sanctuary I felt the crisp, electric, dynamic presence of the Holy Spirit. Everyone could sense that God was up to something. After a powerful worship time, Pastor Jack invited one pastor from each congregation to come up on the enormous stage at the front of the sanctuary. After the entire platform was completely filled with people, Pastor Jack asked each pastor to say a prayer for the city in their native language. There must have been over 30 languages represented.

The power of the Holy Spirit was so evident in each prayer that, whether it was in a language you were able to understand or not, you could sense something earth-shaking was happening. Many of us could not stop tears from flowing because in this giant, sprawling, strife-torn, racially divided city, seeing people representing all cultures, races, and denominations uniting in prayer to bring down the strongholds of darkness that had been erected in the city was transforming and healing. I remember thinking, *This is what the body of Christ is going to look like in heaven.*

"There needs to be leadership in the church body of Christ to help erase the entrenched bitterness in sectors of our society," said Pastor Jack. "There must be a break-through in wrong attitudes, led by the people of God, because nobody else can lead it. We need to start with what people did to the native Americans when this land was settled, followed by what was done with slaves for generations. If you trace it through history, there is no part of our culture that has not been violated. And in retalia-tion, the attitudes that exist in these violated people toward the white culture is just as evil in its own way—a bitterness toward the ones who sowed the seed of evil. There are none guiltless."

In order to cross this great divide in our land, each one of us has to commit to being a reconciler. The way we do that is by first confessing our sins as a people for having violated other people more than we know. Then we must be willing to bridge the breach that has been erected by saying, "God, use me as an instrument to break down all attitudes of hatred, animosity, separation, and disrespect toward other races." And we must also pray together with other believers that there will come the reconciliation and healing needed.

"The breach that came between the tribes of Israel—when the northern tribes divided from the southern tribes—is similar to the tribal warfare that exists in our nation today—all the way from gang wars to the attitudes that exist between ethnic groups," said Pastor Jack. "We, the believers in our nation, must pray that God will wake His people out of numbness, spiritual apathy, and sleep in order to understand their role in leading people on the path of reconciliation."

The only way racial and cultural barriers will be brought down is by the church getting down on its knees to pray. Satan, of course, will resist that. He doesn't want us united on this issue. But we can resist him (1 Peter 5:9). We can "be steadfast, immovable, always abounding in the work of the Lord, knowing that your labor is not in vain in the Lord" (1 Corinthians 15:58).

Any time racial and cultural issues separate people, the praying church must take action. In order for there to come reconciliation, there must first come intercession. And it will begin to be noticed when individual churches not only pray but reach out to other churches and people in the community who are different than they are and give something of themselves to them. Let's invite the Holy Spirit to do what He longs to do, and that is to knit us together in a bond of love.

## Breaking Down Strongholds in Your City

At "Love L.A."—that huge meeting of 10,000 pastors, leaders, and members of hundreds of congregations who gathered to pray for the city—one of the specific things we all prayed for that night was an end to gang warfare. The situation was at its all-time worst and dramatically increasing daily, with more and more people being killed in gang-related murders every week. And it wasn't just gang members getting killed. It was innocent bystanders, even babies and children, who were being murdered as well. It was a heartbreaking and gut-wrenching situation that grieved everyone. It was out of control.

As it turned out, the husband and wife who drove me downtown to the meeting that night, David and Priscilla Navarro, were the very ones God used to answer that prayer. David had been a former gang leader himself, but he had received the Lord and been transformed. While attending Church On The Way, he became a pastor-elder and felt led to be a peacemaker with regard to the gang crisis. So he, along with two other former gang members and a pastor, had the full support of Pastor Jack and the church to call for a meeting of the enormous rival gangs of L.A. in order to discuss a cease-fire. The meeting was held in our church sanctuary on a Saturday, having beforehand been bathed in fervent intercession. These men were not only able to bring this dangerous group of gang members together without incident, they also got them to declare a truce among the gangs. It was astonishing.

After that there came an immediate reversal in the killings, and the mood of the entire city changed. In the year following that meeting, there were *no* gang-related murders, and there came much needed peace. No one who was in attendance at that big city-wide prayer meeting that night can ever be convinced that this wasn't a miracle in response to the many different people joining together to pray for the city.

I'm not telling you things about these prayer gatherings or our congregation as if we were extraordinarily accomplished in faith. We were simply God's people in the middle of a city that was racked with racial riots, rampant crime, senseless murder, violent earthquakes, floods, forest fires, drought, and child pornography, and it could seem like the center of hell sometimes. Yet God began to stir in us a love for that city and its people, and a faith that something could change if we would pray.

"We are not wrestling against flesh and blood, but against principalities and powers," explained Pastor Jack.

"If there is anything we understand about the proportion between the hosts of God and the hosts of darkness, it is that, by actual biblical evidence, the hosts of heaven outnumber the hosts of hell two to one (Revelation 12:4). But far more than that, we have committed to seeking the living God, and having joined His side, our power and expectation of victory increases exponentially. Satan knows he has a short time anyway, but as God's people do battle against him, there is the promise that we will overcome the enterprises of his evil strategies."

The victory is the Lord's and the battle is secure, but victory does not happen automatically. We must enter the scene in prayer.

In another of the citywide prayer meetings that Pastor Jack organized, the Lord told this same group of pastors specifically to "pray against the destruction of the city of Los Angeles." Not long after that, three things happened in succession. There were the Rodney King riots, devastating fires, and the Northridge earthquake. During each of those events, by reason of the prayer commitment that had drawn these pastors together, their churches got involved in action and service that clearly became pivotal in helping the whole city of Los Angeles recover from these horrific points of trauma.

One example of the power of praying together—especially in ways the world will usually not notice because of the invisible working of God's hand—related to the way our prayers for the city's weather patterns doubtless changed what otherwise might have happened. This is the way it occurred.

After the riots, which happened in the spring, many people were predicting that the coming summer was going to make the unstable ethnic tension even worse and create a repeat situation of what we had just gone through. People were concerned that as the summer months brought high temperatures, many people without air conditioning would go out in the streets in large numbers and the riots would happen all over again. In response to those predictions, these city pastors felt led to pray that there would be an amelioration of the summer heat. We prayed for that in our individual congregations as well.

Later that spring, I attended the Mayor's Prayer Breakfast in downtown Los Angeles. Pastor Jack led everyone there in a powerful prayer, asking God to give us cool weather that summer. There were more than 1000 people in attendance, and I could sense tremendous fervency and unity in the room as we all prayed for the Lord to bring a cooling of the weather in our city.

As it turned out, that summer was one of the coolest ever in Los Angeles. The marine layer created a summer-long mantle over the city, and the climate was drastically changed. I had lived there for nearly 40 years, and I don't ever remember a summer in L.A. being that cool and pleasant. The prayer of God's people changes things, including the weather. Even Mayor Tom Bradley indicated he believed the moderate weather was an act of God's grace.

"There's a biblical principle that the multiplying of partnership in prayer multiplies the dimension of impact," explained Pastor Jack. "It's taken from the Lord, who said that five will chase a hundred, and a hundred will put ten thousand to flight (Leviticus 26:8). It's not a matter of saying God is obligated because of the number, but there is a penetrating power when there's agreement in prayer. Agreeing is like striking notes in harmony. The words 'one accord' convey the idea of people all having the same temperature—the same degree of passion, the same degree of focus (Acts 2:1; 2:46; 4:24; 5:12). This reality calls us to pray together, believing the same way about what is possible for our cities."

Pastor Jack went on to teach us that in order to reach a harmony—a "one accord"—we need to:

1. define what we're going to pray about and

2. understand the biblical grounds upon which we're expecting those things to happen.

That's what brings focus to our prayers.

"Praying together for your city requires thoughtful, prayerful inquiry of the Holy Spirit's prayer target," said Pastor Jack. "When we join His *prompting* (what He puts on our heart as weighty issues) to His *promises* (what God says He will do when we pray), faith rises and effective prayer is lifted to heaven."

Through prayer, God has called us to overcome adversity and take dominion over and govern the affairs of earth. Our call to govern is not so much in the sense of political government, but to govern in the spiritual sense of praying "Your kingdom come. Your will be done on earth as it is in heaven" (Matthew 6:10). This is true even if we live in a city that deserves the judgment of God. The Bible gives us hope to believe that God in His mercy will rescue the city and preserve it from the destruction that's due it, if there can be found people who will pray.

When Abraham prayed for Sodom in order to spare his nephew, Lot, and Lot's family, he asks God if He would spare it for the sake of 50 righteous people. And God says He would. He asks if He would spare it for the sake of 45. And God says yes. He asks about 40. Thirty? Twenty? Ten? And the Lord says for the sake of ten, He would spare it. God never stopped saying yes until Abraham stopped asking. It was because there could only be found *four* righteous people that the city was destroyed (Genesis 18:16–19:29).

"Listen to the heart of God in this story," said Pastor Jack. "Is God anxious to wreak judgment on humanity? No. He *was* not, and He *is* not. That was a culture that stood as the symbol of the most perverse, anti-God city in the Old Testament Scriptures. So much so that the traits of Sodom have become a word to describe human and cultural perversion. Still, in that environment the Lord says He would save it for ten people. Let's remember that—and remember that God stopped conceding only when Abraham stopped asking."

How often do we do that too? How frequently do we stop asking God to pour out His Spirit on our cities and do wondrous works of salvation and restoration in the people who inhabit them? If Abraham would have asked more, could Sodom and Gomorrah have been spared? Perhaps. But in any case, the Bible shows that God is waiting to find intercessors, and nothing in our cities is going to get better apart from a praying church.

No matter what city you are living in, God has called you to pray for it. The Bible says, "Seek the peace of the city where I have caused you to be carried away captive" (Jeremiah 29:7). Let's do that. Let's pray together for the peace of our cities. And let's become the powerful praying church God has called us to be.

## Prayer Power

Lord, help me to be a person who reaches out to touch others with Your love. Enable me to extend myself across cultural barriers, racial barriers, denominational barriers, and even church barriers. Help me not to be a person who looks suspiciously at people who are different than me, but rather help me to appreciate differences as one would appreciate the beautiful colors of a rainbow. I pray that I will never withdraw and separate myself from people who are not like me. Teach me instead the best way to reach across dividing lines in love.

Help me to always be in the church You want me to be in, so that I can become a part of the work You are doing there. I pray that I will always belong to a church that worships Your way. One that teaches Your Word in a clear and balanced way and understands the power of prayer. Guide the pastors and leaders of my church to be the men and women of God You created them to be. Help them to clearly understand the path You have for them. Help me and the rest of the congregation to catch their vision and do what is needed to support them. Help us as a people to see Your mission for our church and get behind it wholeheartedly.

Help me to move in unity with my church family and enable us all to move together in harmony. Where there is any kind of disunity, I pray You would bring peace and understanding to bear upon it. Bring redemption and restoration where it is needed. Thank You that You are greater than any difficulty we might face, and Your love guarantees that we will triumph over it.

Help me to be a praising person and teach us as a church to be a worshiping people. Instruct us in what we need to know about worship and prayer so that we can become the intercessors You have called us to be. We worship You because "You are worthy, O Lord, to receive glory and honor and power" (Revelation 4:11). I know it is good to give thanks to You in all things, Lord (Psalm 92:1) for this is Your will (1 Thessalonians 5:18).

Lord, I pray that You would pour out Your Spirit on my church. May each church in my city hear Your call to prayer and take their place to become Your powerful praying church. I pray that all the churches will reach out to one another in love and join together in prayer for our city. May Your love overflow from each church to people everywhere, so that they will be welcoming places of refuge for the lost and hurting. May each church welcome people from every race, culture, color, and background.

Lord, I invite You to reign in this city. Pour out Your Spirit upon everyone so that all people will be drawn to You. Bless our city by exposing all the plans of darkness to Your light so that no establishments of unrighteousness will prevail. Remove the strongholds of evil from our city so that there will be an end to crime, murder, perversion, and wickedness. Make our streets safe from accidents and evil people. Bless the children of our city. Expose anyone who would try to do them harm so that evil people may be removed. Remind me to pray for my city often, and show me how I can join in prayer with others to pray as well. Far be it from me that I should sin against You by not praying for my city (1 Samuel 12:23).

Thank You, Lord, that You have made us to have dominion over the works of Your hands and You have put all things under our feet (Psalm 8:6). Help us to learn to take dominion in prayer as You have asked us to do. Help us to not be afraid when bad things happen, knowing You are our refuge and our strength, a very present help in trouble. Even if the world falls apart, even though the mountains are carried into the midst of the sea, we don't have to fear. Thank You that when we seek You and search for You with all our heart, we will find You (Jeremiah 29:13). Raise us up to be Your powerful praying church. In Jesus' name I pray.

～  ～  ～

## Word Power

Take the helmet of salvation, and the sword of the
Spirit, which is the word of God; praying always
with all prayer and supplication in the Spirit,
being watchful to this end with all perseverance
and supplication for all the saints.

EPHESIANS 6:17-18

Christ[,] from whom the whole body, joined and knit
together by what every joint supplies, according to
the effective working by which every part does
its share, causes growth of the body for
the edifying of itself in love.

EPHESIANS 4:15-16

Your heavenly Father knows that you need all these
things. But seek first the kingdom of God and
His righteousness, and all these things
shall be added to you.

MATTHEW 6:32-33

Far be it from me that I should sin against the
LORD in ceasing to pray for you.

1 SAMUEL 12:23

Yet in all these things we are more than conquerors
through Him who loved us. For I am persuaded that
neither death nor life, nor angels nor principalities
nor powers, nor things present nor things to come,
nor height nor depth, nor any other created thing,
shall be able to separate us from the love of God
which is in Christ Jesus our Lord.

ROMANS 8:37-39

# Six

# Uniting in
# Prayer to Move
# a Nation

A significant turning point in our congregation's life happened on a Wednesday night in November 1973, at a time when everything in our nation seemed out of control. The war in Vietnam and the horrible campus riots in protest of the war had been tearing the heart of our country for some time. Certain newspaper columnists, who usually did not make spiritual observations, said America's soul was at a stress point similar to that which the country experienced during the Civil War. There was even an article in a prominent newspaper that read, "Will America Live to Be Two Hundred?"

The nation was also in the middle of the Watergate crisis, and everyone had unsettling doubts about the future of the presidency. In the prayer meeting on that particular Wednesday night, a young man sang a song the Lord had given him, inspired from the book of Nehemiah in the Old Testament when the people gathered at the Water Gate.

The Water Gate was one of a number of gates constructed into the wall around the city of Jerusalem. But the wall had been broken down and its gates burned when Nebuchadnezzar destroyed the city and took the Israelites into exile. Years later, after some of the exiles returned, Nehemiah, who had become the cupbearer to the king of Persia, heard that the wall still had not been rebuilt. It grieved him so much that he wept and mourned for many days, fasted and prayed before God, and confessed the sins of the children of Israel, who had not kept God's commandments.

Nehemiah sought permission from the king to return to Jerusalem in order to rebuild the walls. Once permission was granted, he went there and organized the people to do the rebuilding work. When the repairs were finally made, the people gathered together in front of the Water Gate to read the Book of the Law and worship God (Nehemiah 8:1-6).

The song the young man sang that night at our church called for the people (us) to gather around the Water Gate (referring to the Watergate crisis in our nation) to worship God, declare His Word, and pray. If we did that, then God would change things. The Holy Spirit also impressed upon our souls that God was calling us to pray for the turnaround of our nation as though no one else was praying. It's *not* that there would be no one else praying, but we were to pray as *if* that were so.

The word God etched on our hearts that evening was, "If My people who are called by My name will humble themselves, and pray and seek My face, and turn from their wicked ways, then I will hear from heaven, and will forgive their sin and heal their land" (2 Chronicles 7:14). To keep us reminded of that verse, Pastor Jack asked us to meet every Wednesday night at 7:14 to pray specifically for the nation.

Beginning with the opening weeks of 1974, we moved forward, praying together as a congregation. We prayed specifically that the Watergate crisis would be resolved, the truth would be revealed, and the right thing would be done.

Pastor Jack also began regular in-depth teachings on intercession that were rooted in the discovery he said he was making. Based on 1 Timothy 2:1-4, he noted three important things for us to remember:

1. Intercession and prayer for everyone—especially governmental leaders—is an absolute priority assignment given to the church (verse 1).

2. The climate of a culture can be affected by praying this way—even unto "a quiet and peaceful life" (verse 2).

3. The objective of such prayer is the advance of the gospel and the entrance of more and more people into the salvation offered through the grace of God's kingdom purposes (verses 3 and 4).

In short, the banding together of the congregation for the purpose of intercession was viewed as being a divine call, a biblical priority, and a humble privilege.

During that time the same two well-known composers from our congregation whom I mentioned in chapter 1 and who had introduced me to Pastor Jack—Jimmy and Carol Owens—wrote a musical called *If My People*. This stirring work, which was inspired by 2 Chronicles 7:14, spoke of the powerful things that can happen when a people will humble themselves and commit to pray for their nation. It took the words of that verse and drove them deep into our hearts, and we caught the vision of how praying for our country really *could* make a difference.

Terry, my singer friend who led me to the Lord, and I, and many other Christian singers, recorded this musical, and a sizeable group toured the country giving live presentations of it. During that tour over 100,000 intercessors committed to daily, ongoing prayer for the nation.

As we continued interceding for our nation with clear purpose, it seemed as though the more we prayed, the more we found to pray about. Of course we prayed for the president, but we also learned to pray for his vice president, Cabinet members, advisors, and all who gave him counsel. We prayed for all elected officials, judges, justices, and military leaders, as well as our men and women in the military. We read newspapers, listened to the radio, and watched news reports on TV with intercession in mind. *Praying without ceasing didn't seem that hard anymore, because it became the natural outflow of an intercessor's heart.*

Not long after that, things began to turn around in the nation in every way. The truth *was* exposed regarding the Watergate Crisis, and while we were all shocked to see the fall of the president and his men, we knew that the hand of God had preserved the nation and enabled us to remain standing. After the presidential elections in 1976, the headline in the same newspaper that had forecast doom read, "A New Spirit Has Come to America." The publishers of this newspaper were more right than they could possibly know. God's Spirit had come like a refreshing breeze to bring healing in response to the intercession of countless people.

What we never read in the history books is how many times our nation has been powerfully affected because people gathered at crucial times to pray. This nation was founded, established, built, and led by praying people. In the early years, the government leaders specifically *called* for people to pray. For example, when drawing up the Constitution and finding themselves at an impasse because of strong disagreements, George Washington and

Benjamin Franklin called the men to a time of prayer every morning. After their very first morning of prayer, the men were able to come to an agreement and then create a document that has kept our nation strong for over 200 years. They acknowledged they would not have been able to do this without God's guidance.

In another example, at a time of great national stress, Abraham Lincoln called for a national day of fasting and prayer to confess the nation's sins of slavery and pride and to ask God's forgiveness. Within two days after that day of prayer and fasting, everything turned around, and the way was paved for the preservation of the union and the freeing of the slaves.

These are just two of the countless times that are *recorded* of people praying for the nation. God only knows how many more examples there are that are *unrecorded*. The point is that praying for our nation is our heritage. And it is also our privilege and duty. It's not just for pastors and leaders to do in churches and conferences. It's for you and me to do in some way every day. *That's because praying for our nation is not an option. It's a mandate from God.*

## If God's People Will Step into the Gap

Stepping into the gap is not about shopping for clothes in a popular store. It's about standing before God and praying on behalf of other people.

For thousands of years the first line of defense for a city was the large wall that had been constructed around it. A city could not be taken unless that wall was breached. A gap was a breach or break in the wall that needed to be repaired. Any gap not repaired would be a place where the enemy could come in.

*An intercessor is someone who steps into the gap between God's righteousness and man's failure, and through prayer, brings the merits of the cross to bear upon people and situations.*

Intercessors are needed because the world is filled with men and women who don't understand the effects of their own sin. Or they don't understand everything God can do for them, and so they don't know to ask for themselves. They don't realize the extent of God's provision for them, so they need someone who will step into their situation in prayer. And even people who *do* know to pray can sometimes be so overwhelmed by their circumstances that they *can't* pray. They need an intercessor to step into the gap for them too. That's where you and I come in. We can answer God's call and partner in His kingdom purposes by praying for people and situations that need the touch of God.

Pastor Jack always said that one of the saddest verses in the Bible is where the Lord is speaking by the prophet Ezekiel to the people of Israel and explaining why judgment could not be averted on their land. God said, "I sought for a man among them who would make a wall, and stand in the gap before Me on behalf of the land, that I should not destroy it; *but I found no one*" (Ezekiel 22:30, emphasis added).

Isn't it amazing that God could not find even one person to pray on behalf of their country? And so He had to judge the land because of all the evil that went on in it. "Therefore I have poured out My indignation on them; I have consumed them with the fire of My wrath; and I have recompensed their deeds on their own heads" (Ezekiel 22:31).

God is saying that this destruction could have been avoided if He would have found just one intercessor.

"You cannot read these words without being deeply sobered by the inevitability of divine justice being executed," said Pastor Jack. "It's not because God is merciless or vindictive. It's because the judgment which could have been averted, wasn't. And it wasn't averted in a land where people had the benefit of every blessing of God's grace upon them. The folly of the people in that land at the time was that they believed God would tolerate their ongoing commitment to evil. They presumed that, having experienced His favor, they were not accountable to the laws of His divine righteousness and judgment. It was His *chosen* people who rejected the wisdom of His ways and finally brought down judgment upon their own heads."

How can we read what God said and not think of our own country with all of its sins? As surely as there is a law of gravity, there is also a spiritual law of reaping what we have sown. Just because we don't see the law prove itself as quickly and clearly as we see in gravity doesn't mean it does not exist. It's just that the time lapse between what we have sown and what we reap can blind us to that spiritual law's existence.

Bad things don't come from God. They happen because we have sown bad seeds or as a result of the enemy's work. Either way, God gives us the opportunity to avert both of those things by standing in the gap through prayer. In spite of everything that is wrong in our country, we still enjoy the blessings we do because countless people have stood in the gap on behalf of our nation.

When God looked for a person to pray and couldn't find *one,* the land was taken over by enemies. Do you see by this how significant a role each of us can play, as we learn to pray together for the protection of our nation today? As we pray, according to God's Word and invoking God's power as intercessors, we can affect the outcome of events, and there can be an averting of judgment on our land.

"God doesn't say that judgment will *never* come," Pastor Jack explained. "But it can be delayed for the time being. Our call is to answer to our 'hour' in history. We cannot change the past, and we cannot predict the future, but we can answer to the assignment of God's Word and pray with the understanding that we *are* accountable for our generation. In such praying, though we appropriately love our country, we can't guarantee what the future may be. But the promise in 1 Timothy 2 focuses our ultimate concern—that people be rescued from judgment in order that they might be saved through the preaching of the gospel."

Of course, unlike ancient cities of Bible times, we don't have walls around our cities anymore. But we can form and sustain a wall of defense around our nation—a wall of God's righteous power to save and to deliver—by praying together. We can answer God's call to "stand in the gap" and live in obedience to His ways. We can invite God's protective shield over the land and His wall of merciful grace around it. But if this shield or wall of prayer is not completely raised, the judgment that is due can break through. We need to understand that it will be everyday people—people like you and me—who will make the difference as we stand in the gap and pray.

## If God's People Will Have Eyes to See

Not long ago a horrible hurricane was predicted off the coast of Florida. It was feared that it would devastate everything in its path, but countless people prayed, and it turned out to be nothing but a rainstorm. Sudden reversals like this happen with no explanation whatsoever, and we must not think for a moment that they are all just coincidence. How many times have we read in a newspaper the words, "It's a miracle"? And how often is that more the truth than most people know? As Scott Bauer, Pastor Jack's successor at Church On The Way, put it, "When God's people intercede, the headlines you *don't* read today [of devastation or destruction] are because of the intercession God's people made the day before."

Our nation, and probably every nation on this earth, is deserving of God's judgment. Yet we haven't seen it in a way we deserve because of the prayers of faithful intercessors. Sin increases in our land with each passing day. Who isn't shocked by new levels of depravity we read or hear about in the media? Still, more and more people are understanding the power of prayer and intercession and are learning how to move into it in a way that is making a difference. Most people don't realize the countless blessings we enjoy in this nation because people are praying.

God is looking for *more* people who will step into the gap in prayer. He is looking for *more* people who will open their eyes to the invisible realm and see what He wants to do in our world today.

When we are blinded to the truth, we miss the mark. We start to grumble and become fearful. How often do we complain about things that are going on in our nation instead of praying about them? How many times do we get nervous, anxious, or worried about what we fear *might* happen instead of committing the situation to prayer? How frequently do we let the blatant proliferation of evil get us down until we feel powerless and overwhelmed in the face of it instead of praying? How often do we feel that prayer requires too much of us, and besides, it just feels good to complain? How much easier is it to blame God, politicians, or the president for what happens in our nation than it is to pray? How often do we think, *My prayers won't make a difference,* instead of asking God to open our eyes to the truth of the invisible realm?

There is a spiritual force that opposes the things of God. Even though we don't see it in the natural, this force can be spiritually discerned through God's Word and as we pray for revelation. There is *another* force that is spiritually discerned too. In the Old Testament, the prophet Elisha and his servant saw that an army had completely surrounded the city with horses and chariots.

"What shall we do?" asked his fearful servant.

"Do not fear, for those who are with us are more than those who are with them," Elisha answered. "Lord, I pray, open his eyes that he may see."

"Then the LORD opened the eyes of the young man, and he saw. And behold, the mountain was full of horses and chariots of fire all around Elisha" (2 Kings 6:16-17).

We need to pray that God will open our eyes to see how He protects us. We need to see the truth about God, the truth about ourselves, and the truth about the enemy so we can pray with confidence, boldness, and faith.

Too many people are lured into prayerlessness by a fatalism they think is scriptural. "Qué será será" is not found in the Bible, yet some of us live as though it is. Yes, the Bible says that in the last days things will become worse and worse. But it doesn't say, "Whatever will be, will be." Or "just let what is going to happen happen." Jesus emphatically said that we don't know the "day or the hour" when God will terminate His merciful season of grace toward humankind. None of us knows whether the end will be in our lifetime or not. But we do know this: Jesus told us to occupy until He comes. He made it clear that we are not to sit back and do nothing. Occupying means keeping our eyes open for ways to pray and doing the work God has called us to do. If we stop praying, who knows what needless suffering will come to us, to those we care about, and to countless others we don't even know?

God tells us that we don't have because we don't ask (James 4:2). It can't get clearer than that. We are supposed to ask God for things that we see need to happen, not because *He* can't see them, but because He has assigned us as intercessors—people who stand before Him on behalf of earthly need to invoke heaven's power and grace. And that is never more clear than in regard to our nation. This is true no matter what nation you are in. And if we don't know *how* to pray, we can ask the Holy Spirit to give us understanding, wisdom, insight, knowledge, and direction in prayer. He will do that and then help us see the *root* of the problem so we're not just praying about symptoms. But we have to ask God to open our eyes to see the truth.

## If God's People Will Answer the Call

The greatest recent awakening to pray for our nation took place on September 11, 2001, when the United States was attacked by terrorists. God had been calling us to prayer all along; it's just that many of us didn't hear it until then.

At about 3:30 A.M., in the early hours of the morning before the World Trade Center was hit by the hijacked planes, I woke up with feelings of overwhelming oppression, sadness, and dread. I knew God was calling me to pray, so I prayed for my family and people I cared about or thought might need prayer. I prayed for the president because I pray for him every day. But beyond that I didn't know what else to pray over. I didn't hear the call to pray for the nation because I had gotten out of the habit of praying that way. My mind and heart were just not there. And I knew better.

Of course I started praying the moment I heard what happened, as did people all over the county. And I have no doubt that those collective prayers saved lives that morning and kept the situation from being any worse. But I regret that I didn't hear the call and stand in the gap earlier.

Just as God called Nehemiah to go to Jerusalem and repair the wall, God is calling us to stand in the gap in order to repair the breach in the protective wall around our nation too. Just as they used to put watchmen on the walls to look out for coming enemy attacks, God is calling us to be His watchmen on our nation's walls.

Nehemiah answered the call at great danger to his life. It was risky to ask if he could rebuild a city that had once been a source of great irritation to the king. We may not be risking our lives the way Nehemiah did, but being a watchman requires something of our lives in terms of commitment and time. Nehemiah's concern for the people of the city motivated him to pray. Our love for the people in our nation should motivate us to pray too. We need to be so heartbroken over the brokenness of people that we think more about their well-being than we do about our convenience.

"One of the hindrances to intercessory prayer is ignorance of the church's collective mission, which is the call to prayer," said Pastor Jack. "There is woven into the fabric of man the supposition that the die is already cast, that there's some cosmic arrangement of things, and the best you can do is try and cope with it the way it's going to be. But Jesus taught exactly the opposite. There is nothing whatsoever anywhere in the Bible that suggests that man is the victim of an irretrievable circumstance. The whole concept of redemption argues against that. Christ's coming and reversing the power of death—transforming the future by His resurrection—is in itself a statement that nothing is irredeemable. But His action is also a statement that says though things may be redeemed, they are not redeemed without someone stepping in. Just as His 'stepping in' is described as an intercessor's action (Isaiah 53:12), on the grounds of what He achieved through His death and resurrection, we are called to 'step in' to see the power of His triumph applied today."

That's where we come in. We are the intercessors God is calling today. He has made us agents of His kingdom, and He wants us to become His instruments of redemption in every situation through Holy Spirit-energized prayer. If we can get beyond our doubts that prayer doesn't change things and be willing to answer God's call to pray, there is no limit to what He can do in our land.

"God says, 'I'm looking for someone who will be an earthly representative of what has been accomplished through My Son,'" said Pastor Jack. "'But unless it's claimed, I will not change that anymore than I can alter the destiny of the human soul that doesn't receive the salvation My Son has provided.' It's our decision and responsibility, and that's the whole arena so glibly passed over by the church when we misconstrue the grand and wonderful truth of the sovereignty of God.

"God's sovereignty refers to His absolute, irrevocable power as the Ultimate Being, the Almighty God of the universe. It incorporates all the greatness that is inherent in His Person, His power as Creator, and the wonders of the fact that He is all-knowing, all-powerful, and everywhere present. Make no mistake: We strongly assert the great truth of the sovereignty of God. However, for some today, God's sovereignty has come to mean that God arbitrarily or randomly exercises His power; that somehow He has fatefully designed the course of human affairs toward a destiny that involves nothing of human participation. But as earlier mentioned, what God does with reference to earth, He has chosen to do in partnership with humankind who will respond to His love and who will welcome His power and grace into their lives and then into their world.

"Jesus said, 'Here are the keys to the kingdom. You have the privilege of moving in partnership with the Father's kingdom, and whatever you bind on earth is bound in heaven, and whatever you loose on earth is loosed in heaven' (see Matthew 16:19). 'Binding' is when we take action to invoke His rule by revoking the sin or evil workings of flesh or devils. 'Loosing' is when we take action by welcoming His power to release the flow of His mercies and grace into the middle of earth's pain and problems. And all the while, we remember that the power is *His,* but the privilege of tapping into it is *ours.* It's His plan: Without His sovereign power, we can do nothing; without our obedient partnership, He *will* do nothing."

It's like having plenty of money in the bank to cover your bill, but if you never write a check or draw on it when the bill comes due, it doesn't get paid. The authority we have to draw on God's power is ours because of what Jesus did on the cross. We tap into His sovereign power in prayer. We don't determine *what* will be done, because we say, "Your will be done in all things." Yet if we don't hear God's call to prayer and answer it, we miss out on the blessings God has for us.

When Ronald Reagan was elected president, my prayer group and I were strongly led to pray specifically for his safety. We always prayed for whoever was the president, according to God's Word instructing us to pray for those in authority, but this was way beyond what we normally did with regard to that. At first we thought perhaps we felt such a strong connection to President Reagan because he had been a much respected governor in our home state. (Or maybe we had just seen too many of his old movies!) But when the assassination attempt on his life occurred, we *knew* why God had called us to pray. And we believe God called *many* of His faithful intercessors to pray as well. We know it was a miracle in answer to prayer that President Reagan was not killed.

On the morning of September 11, 2001, Pastor Jack was in Williamsburg, Virginia, speaking to about 300 pastors. When they were told that the World Trade Center had been struck by planes, before dismissing the group to return to their homes, Pastor Jack led those leaders in prayer. He sensed God wanted them to do more than pray a desperation prayer born out of shock. God was calling them to fervent intercession with spiritual insight and boldness.

He first asked the group to stand, join hands in faith, and begin to praise God in the confidence that His almightiness was greater than the present moment of fear and tragedy. As he began to pray, he felt the Lord give him a picture of a snake lifting its head, and he saw himself with a sword in his hand.

"Lord, we come against that evil that's seeking to raise its head right now," Pastor Jack prayed. Then he described seeing himself symbolically reaching out with this invisible sword and slashing off the head of that thing, saying, "We come against *any* further incidents of this conspiracy. Things we don't know about yet."

A great number of people besides me heard the call to pray against something more that might occur that morning. The Holy Spirit guided those prayers as well, given the results of one event alone—that of a courageous Christian man, Todd Beamer, who led the resistance that kept a second plane from crashing into the nation's capital. A significant reduction in the destruction that was planned by the terrorists undoubtedly happened as a result of that. How many more things were planned that we don't even know about? And they were stopped because all across the earth believers were praying from the time they saw the first pictures of the burning towers. Because of the intercession of believers in the midst of that hellish assault, less than 3000 people died that day when it could easily have been ten times that many.

Today the threat to our country is great. We can't afford to ignore that we have a formidable enemy who hides and waits to suddenly appear and try to destroy us. The Bible says, "Unless the LORD guards the city, the watchman stays awake in vain" (Psalm 127:1). The security systems we have in our country function in vain unless the Lord keeps watch over the nation. We have to hear God calling us to pray for the protection of our nation and the safety of its people.

*Many are called, but few are listening. Be one of those who is listening.*

## If God's People Will Humble Themselves

One of the most important things that Nehemiah did as he mourned the condition of the city and the people was to *confess the sins of the nation* (Nehemiah 1:1-11). God is asking us to do the same. God wants our hearts to break for the people of our country too. He wants us to humble ourselves before Him and confess the sins of our land so He can heal the breaches in the walls of our nation.

You may be thinking, *Why should I have to confess the sins of other people? I didn't commit them.* But confessing the sins of other people is not like saying, "*I* did it and they *didn't*." It's saying, "I acknowledge their actions as sin against You and I confess it because they won't or don't know how."

We Christians can become self-righteous if we believe that because we have been forgiven of all of *our* sins, then we no longer need to be identified with the people in our nation who haven't. But the prophets in the Bible always identified with the sins of their people. They lived God's way, yet they had to confess the sins of those who didn't. It's important to remember that "If we confess our sins, He is faithful and just to forgive us our sins and to cleanse us from all unrighteousness" (1 John 1:9). Confession is the only way our nation can be cleansed from the effects of sin.

When Promise Keepers met on the Mall in Washington, DC, to pray for the nation, Pastor Jack was asked to serve as the "pastor" of the event—leading the whole day, not only as one of the speakers but assisting to coordinate and sustain focus for the more than 1 million men who were there from across the nation. In drawing them and the national television audience together, he said, "We didn't come to seize Washington by the throat with a political agenda. Instead of coming to take Washington, we came to be taken by God. We came to be delivered first from our *own* sins so that we could offer an incense of righteous worship to Him. We wanted to ask God to have mercy upon our land so that our nation could avoid certain judgment. We wanted there to be set in motion a stream of grace that would transform our nation. We knew that prayer, praise, and confession is the key to putting it in process."

There is plenty to confess each day in our land. Every one of us who knows what this nation *could* be has a sense of loss over the moral decay in this country. We have become a people who can't even distinguish between right and wrong. But Pastor Jack always advised us to "focus on the promises of God, and not on the problems; focus on the Savior's victory, and not on the adversary's actions; focus on our privilege in prayer, and not on our inadequacy; focus on humility in spirit, and not on anger over surrounding sin; and focus on identifying with the sinful, and not on their guilt or failure." So while we need to *confess* the sin, we don't need to *focus* on the sin. We should instead focus on the *sinner,* who needs to be free of his sin by coming to the Lord, and we should do so without condescension or self-righteousness of attitude, but with compassion and humility.

"Except for God's grace, we are altogether a sinful and rebellious people who don't want to acknowledge God or live His way, so let's keep that in mind when we pray for our nation and its sin," said Pastor Jack. "We are such a privileged nation in so many ways, you would think we would constantly be praising God and thanking Him for His grace and undeserved goodness. But we lead the world in corruption. We produce most of the trash that shapes corrupt thought and practices in the world. We're the best market for this trash, and also we're the best resource for marketing the same. What we produce is media trash, and what we procure is chemical trash. And in the wake of it all there is no reason to claim we deserve anything else than the judgment of God, except...except our hope in His promise that if people will humble themselves and confess the sins of the nation and pray, He will extend mercy."

Does that mean if we can confess the sin of child pornography, God will stop it? With God anything is possible. But even if God doesn't stop the entire pornography market overnight, we *can* expect that every confession we make and each prayer we pray *will* affect something or someone. If our confession and prayer would save one child from being violated or would expose the sins of one pedophile, it would have accomplished something great. We may never know what God will do in response to our confession and prayer. But we will certainly see the results of our *not* doing it.

## If God's People Will Enter the War

Ever since September 11, 2001, our nation has been at war, for the most part fighting an enemy we can't always see. We are blessed to have a strong military force that we are proud of and thankful for, who will do everything they can to keep our country safe. But God wants *each one of us* to become a member of an army. *His* army!

God is Commander-in-Chief of this army, and the weapons of choice are prayer, praise, and the Word of God. That's because "though we walk in the flesh, we do not war according to the flesh. For the weapons of our warfare are not carnal but mighty in God for pulling down strongholds" (2 Corinthians 10:3-4). No enemy can stand against these weapons, unless, of course, the enemy convinces us that our weapons are powerless and we stop using them.

*Principalities* and *powers* are terms in the New Testament that are used to describe invisible demon powers that resist the purposes of God on earth. As people come under control of this realm of darkness, you and I have been given the power through the cross of Christ to pray against the plans of evil. We make war against this evil force in prayer.

God's army is an all-volunteer organization, so we have to enlist. We have to tell God we want to be a part of His army of prayer warriors and ask Him to put us on high alert so we can be mobilized at a moment's notice. The best part about being in God's army is that He goes with us into every battle. He says, "Today you are on the verge of battle with your enemies. Do not let your heart faint, do not be afraid, and do not tremble or be terrified because of them; for the LORD your God is He who goes with you, to fight for you against your enemies, to save you" (Deuteronomy 20:3-4). He says all we have to do is pray, worship Him, and declare His Word, and He will do the rest for "the battle is the LORD's" (1 Samuel 17:47).

You may be saying to yourself, *How can I make a difference? I'm just one person.* But when Samuel prayed on behalf of Israel as the Philistines attacked them, "the LORD thundered with a loud thunder upon the Philistines that day, and so confused them that they were overcome before Israel" (1 Samuel 7:10). Every prayer you pray brings confusion upon the enemy too.

God is asking so little from us in terms of the sacrifice of time. One easy way to start fitting intercessory prayer for our nation into your day is to pick up your newspaper or turn on a news report on the TV or radio and choose one or two of the news items to pray about. You'll have plenty of choices. Then let the Holy Spirit lead you from there. Remember, everything that happens in our nation affects each of us personally in some way. That's why, when it comes to praying for the country we live in, we can't afford not to.

The great thing about praying for your nation is that you are never praying alone. That's because you have become part of the army of prayer warriors who are *always* praying. There are even a number of national prayer organizations you can join. Pastor Jack and I are Honorary Committee Members of one such organization called the Presidential Prayer Team (www.presidential-prayerteam.org). Some of the other members are Franklin Graham, Joni Eareckson Tada, Michael W. Smith, Dr. Lloyd Ogilvie, Rebecca St. James, Lisa Beamer, Luis Palau, A.C. Green, John C. Maxwell, Kay Arthur, Thomas Kinkade, J.C. Watts, and James Robison, to name a few. There is no charge to become a member, and you will be notified every week about strategic ways you can pray for the president and the nation. It can't get any easier than that. Please come and stand in the gap with us.

"We're not going to change our nation by means of political strategies," said Pastor Jack. "The nation will only be changed in one realm, and that is the spiritual realm. That's why the Bible says we're not wrestling with flesh and blood. The best political agenda is limited, though we're thankful when godly leaders serve in public office. But prayer alone will bring a spiritual renewal that will change this country. We need to move as people who recognize our time has come and say, 'God, we will take this hour, this moment, and move in prayer with power.'"

God says our prayers can change things by casting out evil and replacing it with His goodness. Yet often we don't keep up on our end of it. We accuse God for what Satan does instead of praying for the plans of the enemy to fail. If the enemy seems to be winning more and more in our land, it's because we have taken ourselves out of the battle by not praying.

"When the Holy Spirit's intercessory call and enablement grips the hearts of believers and out of their inner being flows rivers of living water, a mighty tide of prayer will begin to rise and surge so that the Lord can sweep away the works of darkness that would seek to possess our land," exhorted Pastor Jack.

I know what you may be thinking. *I have a life. I have work to do. I have problems to deal with. I have relationships that are troublesome. I have financial worries. I have health concerns. I have children to raise. I'm just trying to get through my day and pray for myself and my concerns. I don't have time to pray about the nation too. Let other people do it.*

I know how you feel because I have felt the same way. I know the enemy always tries to keep us distracted with one battle after another in our own personal lives. Battles over our finances, our health, our work, our children, our minds, our emotions, our marriages, our relationships, or whatever front he is attacking us on can be so all-consuming that we don't have time for much else. I know that he wants us so preoccupied with our personal battles that we are always fighting defensively. That way he can wear us out.

Where we go wrong is that we fight from battle to battle and never really enter the war. We think that when we win *one* battle we have *won* the war, and so we stop fighting. And on the other side of that, sometimes when we *lose* a battle we feel we have *lost* the entire war, and so we give up. *What we have to realize is that the war is never over!* The triumph Jesus won when He said, "It is finished" (John 19:30), broke the power of sin, death, and hell once and for all. But that victory awaits application on earth—and prayer is the warrior's strategy by His assignment. The conflict will not be over until we go to be with the Lord. That's why we must learn to go on the offensive in prayer instead of waiting until something happens and then trying to defend ourselves.

You know how fervently you pray when something goes wrong in your life? Well, God wants us to pray that fervently all the time. He wants us to intercede every day with the same degree of passion we have when we are in the middle of a crisis. He doesn't want us to just keep losing and regaining the same territory over and over. He wants us to pray in *advance* of disaster so we are not constantly mopping up the mess the devil has made. The peace that God would like to give us depends upon us doing that.

This is worth repeating loud and clear: *THE WAR ISN'T OVER YET!* Let's commit to entering the war for as long as it takes and learn to follow God's orders. Let's stand together with others across this nation and pray, so that God will heal our land.

## Prayer Power

Lord, I thank You for the privilege of speaking to You in prayer. Increase my faith to believe that I can make a difference in my nation when I pray. Help me to comprehend the significance of standing in the gap not only for my family, church, and community where I work and live, but also for my city, state, and nation. Give me direction to know how to intercede in every situation and for every concern. Make me bold to ask. Enable me to ask according to Your will. Give me faith to believe that impossible things can happen when I pray. Forgive me when I have any doubt about Your ability to answer.

I pray for a divine visitation of Your mercy and grace upon my city_____, my state_____, and my nation_____. I declare You to be Lord over these places. It is a privilege to be able to be a part of affecting my city, state, and nation for Your glory. God, help me to understand my role as an intercessor for my country. Help me to be Your instrument of peace, healing, and deliverance. Give me strength to not give up or shrink back when I see enemy opposition. Grow me into being a powerful intercessor who understands the authority I have been given by You in prayer.

I stand in the gap before You on behalf of my country and ask Your forgiveness. Lord, I'm not coming to You on the grounds of our nation's righteousness, but on the grounds that You have given us the privilege to appeal for Your mercy. I come before You and repent of the sins committed in our nation. Specifically I confess the sins of

_____.

Pour out Your mercy upon our land instead of the judgment we deserve. Deliver us from pornography, abortion, murder, stealing, lying, corruption, fraud, destruction, and violence. Keep us from being polluted by all that pollutes our culture, so that we may come before You with pure hearts and clean hands. Expose all sin in us and wash us clean. I am not pleading for Your grace because I think we deserve it. As a people who once knew You, we are worse than nations that sin against You that have *never* known You. But I come because my heart breaks for the brokenness of my nation's people. And I know You are a God who is merciful.

Lord, I surrender any fear and anger in me over the things I see happening in my nation today May these things I see provoke me to pray rather than to criticize, complain, or to withdraw in fear. I know that whatever I ask in Your name, Jesus, You will do, so that the Father may be glorified. Help me not to become more preoccupied with the problems I see than with Your power to change things. Help me to be an instrument of bringing Your power to reign in this land.

Lift the blinders off of us as a nation so that we can see the truth about who You are and what our condition is. Where sin abounds in our nation, may Your grace abound even more. Forgive us for our pride that makes us think we can live without You. Lord, just as You wept over Jerusalem, saying if they had only known the day of their visitation (Luke 19:44), I pray that the believers in this nation will weep over our nation in repentance and recognize the day of *our* visitation. Align our hearts with Yours and heal our land.

Protect our land from being destroyed by the enemy. Bring righteous leaders into the forefront of decision making and give Your wisdom to each one of them. Destroy the strongholds and plans of the enemy *in* this country and *for* this country. Drive back the works of darkness and deliver us from evil. Protect our military leaders and troops wherever they are. Give them revelation, guidance, and favor. Pour out your peace upon our nation.

Raise up an army of prayer warriors who will enter the war for the long haul and refuse to be discouraged in the daily battle against the enemy. Help us to join forces so that the power in our prayers is multiplied. Strengthen us to stay on the offensive and not take ourselves out of the war every time we win or lose a battle. Enable us to be mobilized on a moment's notice so that we can move in unity and by the power of Your Spirit. Help us to understand the powerful weapon we have in Your Word as we move into battle in prayer. If *You* are for us, who can be against us (Romans 8:31)?

Pour out Your Spirit upon this nation. Bring unbelievers to a saving knowledge of Your Son, Jesus. Prosper us and rain Your blessings upon us. Thank You that Your eyes are on the righteous, and Your ears are open to our prayers (1 Peter 3:12). Raise up the effectual, fervent prayers of Your people. May Your love and peace so rise in our hearts that it becomes our greatest testimony of Your goodness. In Jesus' name I pray.

## Word Power

I exhort first of all that supplications, prayers, intercessions, and giving of thanks be made for all men, for kings and all who are in authority, that we may lead a quiet and peaceable life in all godliness and reverence. For this is good and acceptable in the sight of God our Savior, who desires all men to be saved and to come to the knowledge of the truth.

1 TIMOTHY 2:1-4

Now this is the confidence that we have in Him, that if we ask anything according to His will, He hears us.

1 JOHN 5:14

But evil men and impostors will grow worse and worse, deceiving and being deceived. But you must continue in the things which you have learned and been assured of, knowing from whom you have learned them.

2 TIMOTHY 3:13-14

Men always ought to pray and not lose heart.

LUKE 18:1

Therefore, since we are receiving a kingdom which cannot be shaken, let us have grace, by which we may serve God acceptably with reverence and godly fear. For our God is a consuming fire.

HEBREWS 12:28-29

# Seven

# What in
# the World
# Can I Do?

O ne particularly vivid memory stands out in my mind of an incident that occurred in the late 1970s while I was praying with other people at a Wednesday night prayer meeting. We were divided into prayer circles with hands joined, and each of us had been assigned specific things to pray about regarding concerns around the world. I thought I understood the far-reaching power of prayer, yet when it came to praying for things way beyond the borders of my own country, they seemed beyond me. Especially what I had been asked to pray for that night.

"Pray that the Berlin Wall would come down and the people of East Germany would be free," was how the request was worded. *Great*, I thought. *I might as well be asking God to give me beachfront property on Mars or bring Elvis back from the dead.*

I didn't know how to even formulate such a prayer and still sound intelligent. I struggled a little with it, saying something to the effect of, "Lord, I pray that this wall between East and West Germany will be brought down by the power of Your mighty hand. Make an end to the division of this city and free the people in East Germany from their oppressive rulers."

It almost felt like an empty prayer to me because I could not see the possibility of that ever happening. Although I didn't actually say this, somewhere deep inside my mind I was thinking, "If the Berlin Wall could come down, that would be great, Lord. But I certainly understand how hard that would be."

Over the next few years we prayed about this situation intermittently. But after President Reagan made his famous speech in 1987 challenging Mikhail Gorbachev to "tear down this wall," we prayed more fervently. It seemed as though the more we prayed about it, the more I carried a burden for the people of East Germany and the Soviet Union. My heart broke for them because they were not even free to worship God. In fact, I couldn't get the vision of the wall and the people out of my mind, proving once again that the more you pray for people, the more you grow to love them.

The probability of that wall coming down seemed so remote and impossible to me that I cannot even describe how astonished I was when, two years later, it did. And so easily too. No bombs required. No storming the wall with troops. No mass murders. No war. Just a major miracle. That's all. An inside job. The strength of that iron curtain and the people who defended it were so compromised and weakened by the prayers of the saints that, when pressure was applied, it crumbled.

That event transformed my prayer life with regard to having faith in the power of prayer to effect change in the world. Again, I knew we were not the only ones praying because God calls many. But I knew that our little band of intercessors was not praying with the thought that we had joined a group of millions. We simply prayed *as if* no one else was. And God grew our faith to believe that what we were praying for could actually happen. I learned that our prayers are not diluted because we are praying about people and situations in places that are *far away*. God is always *near* to hear, and that's all that matters.

## When God Tells You to Pray

God calls all of us to pray for our world. But in addition to that, He gives each of us promptings we must not ignore. He will bring specific situations, people, or places to our minds and *prompt* us to pray in a certain way if we listen for His instructions. However, He often starts close to home--with the people and issues of our own lives first—almost like an intercessor's training ground. The last time I ignored a prompting by the Lord made an indelible impression upon my mind, and I regretted it so much that I have never ignored such a prompting again.

This is the way it happened.

My husband, Michael, frequently hires musicians to play on his recording sessions, and he hired one of the best trumpet players in Los Angeles named Paul to play on an album he was producing. During the week of sessions, Paul and his wife invited us to their house for dinner. Through the course of the evening we got better acquainted, and I could sense the need for God in their hearts. But I had not known the Lord that long, and Michael and I had only been married about a year. Plus, they were more *his* friends than mine, and it was also a business relationship. So I was hesitant to say anything about the Lord until I got to know them better.

A few days later they were on my heart in a very strong way. In fact, I could not get them out of my mind. I specifically felt I needed to talk to them about the Lord and invite them to church with us. All afternoon they continued to weigh heavily on my spirit, yet I didn't feel that I knew them well enough to just pick up the phone and call them. I still had little faith in my ability to hear from God at this early stage in my walk. And although I had been in numerous prayer meetings at the church where we learned to intercede for other people in other places, I hadn't stepped into doing it with any consistency on my own.

As the prompting persisted, I decided that the next time I saw Paul and his wife, I would definitely share the Lord with them. But that day never came.

The following morning we received a call from a mutual friend telling us that Paul had died in the night from a heart attack. He was in his early forties and had no history of the heart disease that killed him. We were shocked—especially because we had been with him just a few days before and he seemed fine. It sickened me to think how strongly he had been on my heart, and I deeply regretted that I hadn't called him.

Since that time I have tried my best to not ignore a prompting from the Lord. I have received countless such promptings to pray for others over the years, and I try to respond to each one of them. Now whenever someone even comes to my mind, I don't hesitate to pray for them. I ask God to bless, protect, and guide them, and as I'm praying sometimes the Holy Spirit will give me a more specific sense of their need. If I wake up in the night with an intense feeling of concern about something or someone, I always ask God to show me what it is I am to pray about. Sometimes I get a clear picture, but often I don't know the specifics. And I don't always see the results of my prayers. But that's okay. I don't need to. It's enough to know that I am obeying God.

Another important incident of being prompted strongly by the Holy Spirit to intercede happened in one of my early morning devotional prayer times. I was praying for Paster Jack and Anna. A few months prior to that, I had specifically asked God to show me how I could do something good for this wonderful couple as a way of repaying them for all they had done for me. God instructed me to intercede for them every day. As I was doing exactly that on this particular morning, I began to weep.

When I asked God how to pray more specifically regarding them, He impressed these words clearly on my mind: "Satan wants to pierce Pastor Jack's heart."

"Show me how to pray, Lord. Does that mean Pastor Jack will have a heart attack? Help me to understand."

I began to pray for Pastor Jack's heart to be strong, but that prayer felt empty. I knew his physical heart wasn't the correct thing to be praying for. So I asked the Lord, "How does Satan plan to pierce Pastor Jack's heart?"

This time the answer came. "Satan wants to pierce Pastor Jack's heart through one of his grandchildren."

"Which one, Lord?" I inquired again, and immediately a picture of his three-year-old granddaughter, Lindsey, came to my mind.

I vividly remembered an incident when I went to Pastor Jack's house to drop off something for his wife, Anna, and she was there alone taking care of Lindsey. She invited me into the kitchen, where I put my package down on the table. As I talked with Anna, who was holding Lindsey, I suddenly saw Lindsey's face light up. It was as if a switch had turned on a lightbulb behind her eyes, and her face became animated by a giant smile. I turned around to see what on earth could have captured her interest so profoundly, and I saw that it was her grandpa, Pastor Jack. He had come home and quietly entered the hallway behind us. When Anna put Lindsey down, Lindsey ran full speed toward him, and he lifted her up in his arms. This memory convinced me that something happening to *any* of his grandchildren would definitely pierce his heart. Yet I wasn't positive that this prompting was only about Lindsey, so I prayed for God's protection over of *all* of his grandchildren.

When I still did not feel released from the burden of praying for them, I told my husband what was happening. "Do you think I should call Pastor Jack and tell him about this?" I asked.

"Yes, call right away," he insisted.

I dialed Pastor jack's office and not his home because I didn't want to worry Anna in case I was wrong and this was all nothing. At the same time, this kind of thing had never happened to me before with this kind of urgency, so I knew I needed to follow God's prompting.

"I'm not positive it's Lindsey or if she just came to my mind because I have seen her most recently," I explained, "but I haven't been able to stop praying or crying about this, and the Lord wouldn't give me any peace until I told you."

When I got off the phone, I finally felt totally relieved of the burden and was able to get on with my day. I didn't even think about it again until weeks later when Pastor Jack told me that he had called the entire family together that same afternoon to pray for *all* the grandchildren, with particular emphasis on Lindsey.

"Several weeks had passed since our family had gathered to pray over the grandchildren, and, though we were still praying, the tenseness of the warning did not seem as prominent," he said. "This occurred in November, and because the Christmas season was approaching, I decided I needed to clean out our garage. I was just finishing the job when Scott and Becki (Lindsey's mom and dad), along with their three children, stopped by. Scott helped me as I finished cleaning in the garage, while Becki and the children visited with Anna in the house. Somehow Lindsey drifted back outside.

"Because our heavy two-and-a-half-car-wide garage door had a broken spring, I had propped it open with a pole. But now, having finished the sweeping up, I gave one last glance around to make sure that everyone was out of the way before I dropped and closed the heavy door. I knocked away the pole, and just as the mammoth door came thundering down, from out of nowhere Lindsey walked around the corner of the garage and stood underneath the falling door, which was moving directly toward her head."

In an instant, Pastor Jack reached out and caught the massive door and pushed the pole back in place to prop it open. He swept Lindsey up into his arms, trembling with shock as his eyes filled with tears.

"It is absolutely miraculous that I caught it!" he said. "In one revealing instant I knew what had happened. I turned to a shaken Scott with my eyes brimming and said, 'That was it! That was what the Lord was warning us about!' Believe me, we had a praise session!" Each one of us recognized that God had used Holy Spirit-prompted warnings to bring us to vigilant prayer. Such warnings tend to frighten some people, but God's workings are not something to be feared. Warnings are not bad omens. Neither are such warnings to be seen as God's way of letting us know in advance of something evil He has predestined. The Father does not plan evil things to happen to us, but His Spirit warns us of calculated attacks by the enemy. In this instance I have no question whatsoever that God's grace and wisdom prompted a response which preserved the life of our granddaughter."

If I had not interceded for Pastor Jack and his family that day the way the Holy Spirit directed me to, if I had not called Pastor Jack to tell him about it, if he had not taken it seriously and called the family to pray together that day, God only knows what might have happened. I'm not saying it's all our fault if something bad happens to someone and we didn't pray, but I believe God prompts many of us to pray specifically. Unfortunately, few of us trust that we are really hearing from God, and so we don't respond with prayer.

"Jesus said that all power in heaven was given to Him, and on the cross He broke all the power of hell and rendered powerless all works of the flesh," explained Pastor Jack. "He put those powers of darkness under His feet, but He tells us that if those things are going to be *kept* underfoot, we need to step in and pray. When we see works of hell beginning to break loose and manifest, when we see human flesh failing miserably, God says we have the right to immediately step into that situation in prayer. The intercessor stepping in has been given a role, and that is to bring the triumph of the cross of Jesus Christ to bear upon the situation. *Intercession is praying on behalf of another, with the Holy Spirit's direction and enablement, while recognizing all consequences depend on those prayers.*"

Prayer is not guesswork, superstition, or an arrogant assumption that we ourselves are powerful. When people pray, things happen, but the power is God's. Many things happen to people because when they are warned, they *don't* pray. God wants to get our attention so that we *will*.

Whenever you receive a prompting, don't ignore it. God may be telling you to pray. Ask the Holy Spirit to show you how.

## When the Issues Are Big and You Feel Small

If you are like I was, when it comes to praying for the world you might be thinking, *The issues in this world are so enormous and I am so small. Who am I to ask for such big things? Who am I to think that I can actually make a difference when I pray about important and seemingly impossible issues?*

If you have ever thought that way, let me encourage you. You serve a big God. You don't need to become intimidated by the grand scope of the things you pray about.

They may be bigger than *you* are, but they are never bigger than *God* is.

"There is another realm of intercession that reaches out further than most people realize they have the privilege to do," Pastor Jack explained. "If you suggest to the average person that they can pray for nations in other continents, it seems too gargantuan to be real. There is a dearth of understanding among people in general as to the place and the power of prayer. So many people think only mystical or ethereal thoughts about prayer. They think of prayer as a kind of noble attitude that somehow generates or emanates an invisible power. More than being *God's* power, I believe prayer is often seen as a kind of 'force' that might float around and possibly—maybe—envelop someone with a 'positive influence.'

"However, the kind of prayer the Bible reveals—the praying that Jesus calls us all to do *together*—is a God-given means to touch the core of His divine purposes so that they resonate in the human circumstance. Again, He invites us—no, *calls us*—to partnership in the release of those purposes. Frankly and simply put, there are certain things that won't happen unless people pray."

The great comfort in praying for the world is remembering that we are not alone. I might feel weak in the face of giant issues of prayer, but when I know that there may be thousands—even millions—of others joining with me, and we are in essence praying together, it gives me boldness and increased faith.

The good news is that you can start small. You don't have to pray for the whole world in a day. You don't have to begin by praying for the Western Hemisphere or the entire continent of Asia. You can start in your own world. The world you know about. Pick a nation, a city, an area, a people group, a person, or a situation you are familiar with, and pray about something specific regarding that.

Ask the Holy Spirit to help you, because "the Spirit also helps in our weaknesses. For we do not know what we should pray for as we ought, but the Spirit Himself makes intercession for us with groanings which cannot be uttered" (Romans 8:26).

Pastor Jack told us that in his first week as pastor of our church, there were only six people at the midweek prayer service. They all sat in the second and third rows on one side of the small sanctuary. When it came to the prayer time, he asked the small group for prayer requests.

"Let's pray about the earthquake in Guatemala," said one of the men.

"Well, what should we pray?" Pastor Jack asked.

There was a silent pause as they thought about it.

"What more can we say beyond, 'God, help the people in Guatemala'?" he asked the group.

One person spoke up and said, "Let's pray for the people who have been bereaved because of those who have been killed."

"Let's pray for proper medical aid to be given to people who have been injured," said another.

"Let's pray for people to send them aid, like medicine, blankets, and food," said a third.

"Let's ask God to show us what *we* can do to help," said the next person.

"Let's pray that this earthquake will increase people's *desire* for God instead of fueling their *anger* toward God," said another.

As each suggestion came forth, the group ended up with a number of good ways to intercede for this country.

The following week at the prayer meeting, these same people discussed what had happened in Guatemala during the week. There had been news reports about the high efficiency of medical teams during the crisis. Also, government order had been restored to the area so the plundering was stopped. And this prayer group had new compassion for the people there. They had each thought of specific ways they could help the people in Guatemala by sending food and money to organizations that would deliver it. Pastor Jack led the congregation to bring canned foods, blankets, and clothing—items the Red Cross was requesting for Guatemala—to church the following week to give to the Guatemalan earthquake victims. And they responded by giving generously.

In teaching this small group how to pray about large issues, Pastor Jack showed them the importance of recognizing there is more to say in prayer than just, "God, help Guatemala." He taught them how to ask for specific things. And when they saw specific answers to their prayers, their faith was increased.

"I am persuaded that the purposes of God on this earth simply await a praying people," said Pastor Jack. "You may say, 'Well, you don't *just* pray.' And that is correct. But I've never seen people who *really* prayed who '*just* pray.' But I have seen a lot of people who tried to do busy things and *didn't* pray. And the busy things are never as productive as they would have been if they had been predicated upon intercessory prayer."

If the millions of believers in Jesus Christ in this world today would refuse to think small and each one of us would take our place in intercessory prayer daily, even if for only a few minutes, can you imagine the awesome release of power that would begin to sweep the face of this planet as the spirit of God was released to move into areas where there is no penetration point now?

Don't ever be intimidated by the size of the issues God calls you to pray about. Because He is on your side, no force of darkness can resist the power of your prayers.

## When Our Mission Seems Impossible

We've all seen football games where the receiver is running out to catch the ball with the intention of taking it over the goal line for a touchdown. But then suddenly a member of the opposing team leaps in front of him and catches the ball instead and reverses what was once headed a certain direction. The ball is intercepted and the player who intercepted it takes it the *opposite* way. It not only stops what the opponent is doing, but it can reverse the game to become a victory for the other side.

Intercessory prayer does that too. A person—such as you or I—steps in and intervenes. We seize or intercept a situation that is headed a certain way and, by praying, take it the other way to victory.

I remember being in a meeting one time at our church when Pastor Jack told us that missionaries in Bogotá, Colombia, had called, requesting that we pray about what seemed to be an impossible situation. They told us there was going to be a world convention of witches in the city, and they wanted us to pray that God would keep it from happening. We interceded that night in a powerful time of spiritual warfare. It felt to me as though there was overwhelming opposition in the spirit when we started praying, but that heaviness dissipated as we continued to pray and lift up praise to God.

A few days later, the missionaries called us and related what happened when the convention convened. Unexplainably, a huge swarm of bees came into the hotel where it was being held. The bees kept pouring in so fast and in such great numbers that they could not be eradicated. No matter what people did, they were not able to gain control over them. The situation became so bad, in fact, that they had to cancel the entire convention! In relating this after the fact, Pastor Jack noted a passage in the Bible that says, "I sent the hornet before you which drove them out from before you," (Joshua 24:12). He admitted that he hadn't thought about that verse before, but surely God had set a precedent for this to happen again in response to prayer.

What that simple yet utterly profound miracle did to strengthen our faith is recorded for all time in our memories. It reminded us *again* that no matter what a situation looks like, with God nothing is impossible. And we don't have to know all the answers, because God has solutions we can't imagine.

God wants to pour out His Spirit on *all* nations so they can be brought to a saving knowledge of Him. He promises to give us the nations we ask for—even people groups who seem to be impossible to reach with the truth about Jesus (Psalm 2:8). God has not forsaken the nations of the earth. We have forsaken our call to prayer. But as we respond to what the Lord is calling us to pray about, no matter how big or impossible it may seem, there is no limit to what God will do.

## When We Stop Seeing Ourselves as Victims of Circumstance

Pastor Jack taught us that the word *intercede* means "to come upon by chance." The essence of the word "intercede" in both Hebrew (*pahgah*) and Greek (*entunchano*) focuses on the unplanned or seemingly accidental nature of the encounter. Have you ever suddenly found yourself in a difficult situation that you never could have predicted, and you wonder why on earth you are there? Do you realize that perhaps it is to pray? As an intercessor you are never a victim of circumstance. Things just don't *accidentally* happen to you. God foresees every moment of your life, so when you come upon a circumstance that seems disturbing to you, ask God what you are to do about it as *His intercessor*.

"The world is full of things God didn't plan," said Pastor Jack. "It's full of situations that are the result of human sin and failure, not to mention things that are cataclysmic and are no more a part of what God originally intended for this planet than sin. But they are all around us. And we can find ourselves in the middle of a situation that affects us profoundly but is not of our creation at all. If you try to run from the situation, you may be overlooking the fact that the Lord has placed you in the middle of that tough place for a reason. And if you will begin to pray, you can become the instrument by which the climate of that setting will be changed."

Let me give you a very small example of seeing yourself as not just an accidental witness to a situation, but an intercessor who partners with God. As I am writing this very chapter, there is a man outside my window about 20 yards away on my neighbor's property who is up a very tall tree cutting off dead branches. He is making a horrendous and deafening racket with his buzz saw.

I, on the other hand, have a rare morning when everyone in my house is actually quiet and I have the opportunity to think without being interrupted. I had just sat down at my desk and begun to write when the noise of this man's chainsaw began to blare. At first I started to get irritated. I wasn't irritated at the man because he was just doing his job. But I thought, *Why couldn't he be making this noise on a day when I am out doing errands? Why does it have to be on my only quiet morning when I had planned to get a lot of work done in order to meet this looming deadline for which I am painfully behind?*

In the midst of grumbling to myself—which is in essence grumbling to God—the Holy Spirit pricked my heart. Because I am writing this chapter on learning how to pray for others, I remembered that nothing in an intercessor's life ever happens by chance. Obviously I am now being tested by God on this very subject.

"Okay, Lord, I understand what You're telling me," I said as I started praying for the man way up in the treetop. I prayed he would not have an accident with his saw. I prayed he would not slip and fall. I prayed for his life. I prayed for his salvation. The more I prayed for him, the less irritating the noise became. Then I had this thought: Maybe this man is not keeping me from writing my book. Maybe I am here writing my book so that I can pray for *him*.

As an intercessor, God will put you in different situations or allow you to know certain things so that you can intercede. Be aware of that and see what a difference you can make right where you are, simply because you prayed.

## When We Learn to Pray Beyond Ourselves

Several books were written in the late 1990s warning people about the terrible things that might happen in the world when the calendar changed to the year 2000. They took the possibility of what could happen to the absolute limits. But when the calendar turned and the year 2000 came, none of those things happened. Why? Was it because these people didn't know what they were talking about? I don't think so. I think that perhaps some of these writers had a revelation about what the possibilities were, and many of us who had read the books, or heard their predictions, prayed that God would keep those things from happening.

Every week for the entire year preceding the turn of the calendar to 2000, my prayer group and I prayed together about this looming threat. Most of the believers I knew were praying about it. Every praying church I knew of prayed about it as well. There is no way to know for sure, but I believe *nothing* happened because people prayed beyond themselves when they were made aware of what *could* happen.

How many times have serious events been predicted, but they didn't come about because people prayed? We enjoy so many blessings and are protected from far more than we know because of the intercession of believers.

"There comes the prayer that touches the scepter of all power and then things occur," explained Pastor Jack. "The Bible says, 'The effective, fervent prayer of a righteous man avails much' (James 5:16). 'Effective' means that it's energized beyond human energy. 'Fervent' means there is a human passion that recognizes its moment and becomes gripped with a sense of 'I'm here on purpose!' It's recognizing that God is wanting to do something *with* me. I may feel, 'This is way beyond me, but the circumstance *and my ability to address it* is not limited to me, because I know how to pray beyond myself. And if I know how to pray beyond myself, then I can watch God transform situations that are beyond me.' That's intercessory prayer."

Pastor Jack taught us how to pray beyond ourselves for the nations of the world. Because Jesus said, "My house shall be called a house of prayer for all nations" (Mark 11:17), Pastor Jack wanted our church to commit to pray for every nation on the earth. At first that sounded exhausting and impossible, but he encouraged each of us to choose one nation to pray for in an ongoing way. That didn't seem so overwhelming.

South Africa stood out in my mind, and so I chose to pray for that country. I had been there for three weeks in 1968 while I was on a world tour with a singing group that was popular at the time. We agreed to do concerts in Durban, Cape Town, and Johannesburg as long as we could do them for all races. Back then there was a rigid policy of segregation in that country called apartheid. This meant that any race that was not "white" was referred to as "nonwhite" and the two groups were kept separate from one another. They told us that whites and nonwhites would not be allowed in the same building together because it would be too dangerous and people could get killed. So we agreed to do concerts for each group in separate locations.

At a luncheon reception for us in Cape Town, I had the honor of meeting Dr. Christiaan Barnard, who had recently performed the world's first successful heart transplant operation. That was a most remarkable and groundbreaking accomplishment, and now it would be possible for those who faced certain death from heart disease to have a chance to live.

Because our gathering was small and private, I had the opportunity to talk with him briefly. He asked where our group was performing in the different cities, and I told him about having to perform in separate locations to accommodate the apartheid system. I knew he had been trained in the United States, and I thought he would understand the misgivings I felt about the separation of people at our concerts. He *did* understand, but he also explained to me the situation there.

"Nonwhites are about a seventy-five percent majority here," he said. "Whites are a twenty-five percent minority. If apartheid were to end suddenly, there might be a bloodbath. It must be changed peacefully, and we are a long way from that right now."

I got a glimpse of how true his statement was when within a week later, in one of the other towns we were in, a terrible accident happened. We did not witness it firsthand, but we heard about it soon afterward.

The trains in this town were used by nonwhites to get from where they lived to where they worked. But the trains themselves were run by whites. As crowds of people were waiting in the station to catch the next train, it pulled in and accidentally hit a nonwhite man, killing him instantly. Within moments, the nonwhite crowd had pulled the white engineer from the train and killed him. It happened so quickly it was frightening. Everyone knew it was just a drop splashed from a pressure cooker that was about to explode.

That incident affected me so profoundly that years later I wanted to pray for a peaceful end to apartheid in South Africa. This was one of the most beautiful countries I had ever seen. The people there—of every race—were warm, sweet, welcoming, and kind. They were all gripped by a situation they felt very uncomfortable being in, and they needed the grace of God to help them be free of it.

As I started to pray regularly about this issue, another vivid memory of my time spent in South Africa came to mind. I had thought of it often in the years since I'd been there, but now it had new significance to me. It happened the day a couple members of my singing group and I were taken on a trip to the Cape of Good Hope on the southern tip of South Africa, not far from where we were staying in Cape Town. We climbed up to a ridge of rock high above the beach where we could see for miles in all directions. It was a bright, clear, sunny, beautiful, perfect day, and as I stood looking out over the water, I saw where the Atlantic Ocean meets the Indian Ocean. On one side the water was blue, and on the other side it was green. There was a discernable line where the two bodies of water came together. It was magnificent. Breathtaking. Remarkable. I couldn't decide which color was more beautiful.

Now, as I prayed for this country with that vision in mind, I saw the deep racial division as being like these two great oceans. Beautiful colors on both sides, coming together without turbulence, and dwelling beside one another freely and peacefully. "Make these beautiful people groups able to coexist as peacefully and magnificently as these two great bodies of water," I prayed.

I know millions of other Christians prayed about this issue too, especially the many strong and wonderful believers in South Africa. So years later, when I saw the way the apartheid system was dismantled so peacefully, I knew it was a miracle in answer to abundant prayer. It was also a tribute to the greatness of the people in that nation. And it felt good to me that because I prayed, I was a small part of something big that God had done.

I want you to experience that too. I want you to know how exciting it is to pray about something in the world and see God move in response to prayer. I want you to know that wherever you are, you can be part of what God is doing on the earth.

The world needs our prayers more than ever. The battle is not getting easier, it's growing more intense. God wants to raise up His army to become a corporate response to crisis. Our prayers are not going to change God's mind and keep things from happening that He has ordained. But no one knows the timing of certain predicted events. What if these events are not to happen for another hundred years? Sometimes it seems that the world is going downhill so fast that there is nothing we can do except just prepare for the worst and get ready for the Lord's return. But what if the Lord doesn't return in our lifetime? What will the world be like in another 20 years if we don't pray today? How can we just stand by and let people suffer when we have the power to make a difference? We have to remember that no matter how bad things get in the world, they would be a lot worse if no one was praying.

That's why Pastor Jack and I are members of the World Prayer Team (www.worldprayerteam.org). And we invite you to become a member too. Just like the Presidential

Prayer Team mentioned earlier, there is no charge to join, and you will be notified weekly of specific points of prayer. This is especially helpful in times of crisis or major world concerns, which lately are occurring daily. The only way to have a massive prayer meeting is through the Internet, and it can now happen in a moment. In this way we can mobilize a global prayer movement.

"God is always consistent with His own regulations," Pastor Jack said. "By sheer right of His sovereignty He could do anything, anywhere, at any time, by any means. But He doesn't. He confines Himself to the redemptive processes worked though the cross of His Son and released by the ministry of the Holy Spirit throughout the church that His Son redeemed. Let's make no mistake. God's will is clear. He wants us to welcome what He wants to do in our world. He wouldn't have directed us to make the invitation through prayer if it wasn't a necessary part of His purpose and process. Holy Spirit-begotten intercessions forecast new life, new hope, and new possibilities for individuals trapped in the impossible. *Intercession may guarantee someone a tomorrow because we obeyed the Holy Spirit today.*"

One of the countries we prayed about in our weekly prayer meetings at the church was Uganda. It was headed by a brutal dictator, Idi Amin, who eventually killed close to 500,000 of his own people during his reign. The atrocities we kept hearing about caused us to intercede with fervency that God would remove Amin from power and pour His Spirit out upon that nation. It did not happen overnight, but he was eventually removed. Back then a person would be taking his life in his hands by being a Christian. Today over 90 percent of Uganda's approximately 24 million people are Christians. This is absolutely phenomenal. We prayed beyond ourselves, and the answer to our prayers was beyond what we dreamed.

When we all stand together in prayer for our world, we can resist the devil for people who don't know how to do it for themselves. We can bring the strongholds of evil down to nothing. We can love others, weep with those who weep, and cause people to come to a saving knowledge of Jesus Christ. We can help others find deliverance, healing, hope, peace, and joy. We can become an instrument through whom God touches people and situations that we can't even imagine we could ever affect. Each one of us can make a difference when we truly understand and tap into the power of praying together.

What in the world are we waiting for?

## Prayer Power

Lord, help me to have faith to believe that my prayers, along with the prayers of my brothers and sisters in Christ all over the world, will make a difference in the nations. Show me each day which country and which people You want me to pray for. Specifically, I pray for the country of_____.
What I pray for the leader of that country is _____
_____
_____. What I pray for the people of that country is_____
_____.
Lord, I know from Your Word that it is You who raises up kings and removes them (Daniel 2:21). I pray that You would remove all evil and unrighteous rulers and dictators. Raise up godly and righteous leaders to replace them and rule each country. The leaders who are specifically on my heart are_____
_____. Make them to be righteous rulers,

or replace them with rulers who are, so the people in these countries will have peace. Thank You that the work of righteousness will be peace, and the effect of righteousness will be quietness and assurance forever (Isaiah 32:17).

Show us Your ways, O Lord; teach us Your paths. Lead us in Your truth and teach us, for You are the God of our salvation (Psalm 25:4-5). "Let the peoples praise You, O God; Let all the peoples praise You. Oh, let the nations be glad and sing for joy! For You shall judge the people righteously, and govern the nations on earth" (Psalm 67:3-4). Enable the countries of the earth to come together and cooperate peacefully. Specifically, I pray for (name any countries where there is war or civil strife). Bring peace to these nations and people.

Wherever there are people being persecuted for their faith, I pray You would protect them. Break the hold of false religions off of the people who are persecuting them. Specifically, I pray for (name people who need to know the Lord). Pour out Your Spirit in every country and upon the leaders of every government. Reveal the truth of who You are to them. Specifically, I pray that You would send missionaries, evangelists, and Christian workers to (name countries or areas) _____

_____

_____.

Raise up men and women in the body of Christ who will "go into all the world and preach the gospel to every creature" (Mark 16:15). Send messengers and missionaries to tell people who You are and what You have done for them. Pour Your Spirit upon them and anoint them to preach the gospel to the poor. Send them to "heal the brokenhearted," to "proclaim liberty to the captives," and "recovery of sight to the blind." Help them to "set at liberty those who are oppressed" (Luke 4:18). Protect Your servants from persecution. Be with them as You send them to "make disciples of all the nations" (Matthew 28:19). Provide for all their needs.

Lord, You are the light of the world, and I declare You to be Lord over every nation of the earth. I know Your light shines in darkness, even though the darkness does not comprehend it (John 1:4-5), and I know Your light will always prevail. Establish Your kingdom on earth and help us, Your children, to be a people through whom Your light shines and through whom You touch the world for Your glory. In Jesus' name I pray.

## Word Power

Ask of Me, and I will give You the nations for
Your inheritance, and the ends of the earth
for Your possession.

PSALM 2:8

Be still, and know that I am God; I will be
exalted among the nations, I will be
exalted in the earth!

PSALM 46:10

The LORD is high above all nations, His glory
above the heavens. Who is like the LORD our
God, who dwells on high, who humbles
Himself to behold the things that are in the
heavens and in the earth?

PSALM 113:4-6

For the eyes of the LORD run to and fro
throughout the whole earth,
to show himself strong in the behalf of those
whose heart is loyal to Him.

2 CHRONICLES 16:9

See, I have this day set you over the nations
and over the kingdoms, to root out and to pull
down, to destroy and to throw down,
to build and to plant.

JEREMIAH 1:10

# OTHER BOOKS
# BY STORMIE OMARTIAN

**THE POWER OF A PRAYING® WOMAN**
Stormie Omartian's bestselling books have helped hundreds of thousands of individuals pray more effectively for their spouses, their children, and their nation. Now she has written a book on a subject she knows intimately: being a praying woman. Stormie's deep knowledge of Scripture and candid examples from her own prayer life provide guidance for women who seek to trust God with deep longings and cover every area of life with prayer.

**THE POWER OF A PRAYING® WIFE**
Stormie shares how wives can develop a deeper relationship with their husbands by praying for them. With this practical advice on praying for specific areas, including decision-making, fears, spiritual strength, and sexuality, women will discover the fulfilling marriage God intended.

**THE POWER OF A PRAYING® HUSBAND**
Building on the success of *The Power of a Praying® Wife*, Stormie offers this guide to help husbands pray more effectively for their wives. Each chapter features comments from well-known Christian men, biblical wisdom, and prayer ideas.

**THE POWER OF A PRAYING® PARENT**
This powerful book for parents offers 30 easy-to-read chapters that focus on specific areas of prayers for children. This personal, practical guide leads the way to enriched, strong prayer lives for both moms and dads.

**THE POWER OF A PRAYING® NATION**
Learn to intercede in practical ways for our political leaders, military personnel, teachers, and those who work in the media. Affect the strength and spiritual life of our nation through prayer.

**JUST ENOUGH LIGHT FOR THE STEP I'M ON**
New Christians and those experiencing life changes or difficult times will appreciate Stormie's honesty, candor, and advice based on experience and the Word of God in this collection of devotional readings perfect for the pressures of today's world.

# BOOKS BY JACK HAYFORD

## LIVING & PRAYING IN JESUS' NAME

Jack Hayford and Dick Eastman encourage the pursuit of an awareness of Jesus' nature and character through 31 daily studies of His titles and names as revealed in Scripture.

## PRAYER IS INVADING THE IMPOSSIBLE

To Jack Hayford, prayer is not the mystical experience of a few special people, but an aggressive act in the face of impossibility—an act that may be performed by anyone who will accept the challenge to learn to pray.

## LIVING THE SPIRIT-FORMED LIFE

Jack Hayford shows believers how to rediscover the power and blessings of such basic disciplines as prayer and fasting, daily worship, and the release of repentance and forgiveness. Pastor Jack offers an inspiring guide to the Spirit-formed life—where God guides and we thrive.

## PURSUING THE WILL OF GOD

In *Pursuing the Will of God,* Jack Hayford uses the life of Abraham as a template, teaching how God is faithful to reveal His will for our lives as we allow Him to daily lead the way. From career to family, relationships to personal goals, learn to discern and follow God's will for all of the important decisions in your life.

## BLESSING YOUR CHILDREN

Not just for parents, in *Blessing Your Children* Pastor Jack Hayford offers wisdom from the Word about how to influence and nurture the kids in your life, and how to transmit a spiritual inheritance that endures.

## GROUNDS FOR LIVING

With sensitivity, wisdom, and insight, Jack Hayford guides readers through various biblical themes, uncovering truths critical to a steadfast walk with God. *Grounds for Living* covers the doctrines and principles of: the eternal Godhead; the fall of man; God's plan of salvation; grace, repentance, and acceptance; baptism with the Holy Spirit; and what will happen when Jesus comes.

Because principles of pastoral work and leadership of a congregation are discussed so frequently in this book, readers who are pastors or church leaders may be interested in investigating the mentoring resources Dr. Hayford offers in the Jack W. Hayford School of Pastoral Nurture. This auxiliary ministry of The King's Seminary in Los Angeles provides a week of highly interactive leadership-focusing "consultations" each month. Registrants spend six full days with Pastor Jack. Each Consultation is limited to 45 participants. Nearly 2000 pastors from over 50 denominational groups have been involved in recent years. Further information may be found at www.jackhayford.com or by calling 818-779-8047.